BURIED

Navigating the Transitions of Life

Josh Carter

Foreword By
Jim Raley

Buried: Navigating the Transitions of Life
Josh Carter

Famous Publishing
Spokane, Washington

Library of Congress Control Number: 2015939282

Copyright ©2015 Josh Carter

ISBN: 978-1-940243-75-7

Unless otherwise indicated, all scripture quotations designated (NJKV) are taken from the Holy Bible, New King James Version®. Copyright © 1982 by Thomas Nelson, Inc. Used by permission. All rights reserved

"Sanctuary" by Randy Lynn Scruggs and John W. Thompson Copyright © 1983 by Whole Armor Publishing Company and Full Armor Publishing Company. Administered by Peermusic III, Ltd. Used By Permission. All Rights Reserved.

The book you hold in your hands was written from the depths of my heart, out of my personal life and ministry experiences. God inspired me to write it for this exact moment in time. Because of this, I seek only *his* endorsement. It is my prayer that God and his Spirit, power, and presence would back the words on each page.

Undoubtedly, many of my well-qualified friends and mentors would have been willing to write an endorsement for this book, but it was not in my heart to ask them. After much prayer, I was persuaded to offer this book back to God. It is his.

The only other endorsement I would ask for is yours, the reader. If what is on these pages speaks to your heart and spirit, then please share it. It is my prayer that you will share with others this book's impact on you and ministry to you.

Acknowledgments

I would like to thank God for allowing me to write this book that provides readers with valuable information and revelation on the topic of transition. This under-discussed topic is vital to the purpose of God in so many lives today.

I want to thank my amazing wife Natasha for walking with me through our transitions of life and ministry. Thank you for having my back and supporting my ministry and this project wholeheartedly. Without a doubt, you are my "good thing," as the Bible refers to it.

I am beyond grateful to my many mentors and friends—too numerous to list—who spoke life into this project, knowingly or unknowingly. Every phone call of encouragement, insight, and motivation you gave me did not go unnoticed. You all know who you are.

Special thanks to Jim Kochenburger for investing in this project, and to Anderson Bunn for a wonderful cover design. Working on this project with you both has been an incredible journey.

Table of Contents

Foreword

One inescapable fact of life is this: transition. As long as we live, we will endure transition. It starts as a newborn; from the moment we enter the world, we are thrust into the ever-evolving reality of change. From when we are a bright-eyed baby to a silver-haired senior adult, life is all about transition. No one is exempt; it is part of the human condition.

Some transitions are easy, and some are quite challenging. However, when all is said and done, the truth is that perhaps more than anything else, our lives will be marked by how well we handle our seasons of transition. It is amazing to me that while it is such a vivid reality in everyone's lives, transition is actually written and talked about so little in Christian circles.

We can understand the word "transition" in a myriad of different ways. It means, "the process of changing from one condition to another." In life, we can see this demonstrated when young folks get older, unhealthy people become healthy, or someone plagued by bitterness and unforgiveness finds a place of peace through forgiveness. It is a change of condition on a very personal level. It means "to become different" and hopefully better through some sort of transition in one's life. I have finally learned that I do not want to just change; I want to change for the good. The goal of transition is to become better through the process.

I recently wrote a book entitled *Dream Killers*. It is the story of the life of a man named Joseph. If you remember, Joseph was a dreamer. God had showed him a position of honor and leadership. He showed him a place in time when his brothers (who despised and hated him) would actually place him in a position of honor. God basically showed him the palace without showing him the process. He never saw the loneliness of the pit, the humiliation of slavery, or the terror of prison. Joseph could never have imagined the transitions his life would take on the way to his destiny.

God had made Joseph this incredible promise; and when God makes a promise, it is. In other words, if God declares a thing, it is a done deal! What must be understood is this: During the time when Joseph passed through difficult seasons of transition, God was not only preparing the blessing . . . he was also preparing Joseph.

Even in your own personal life, as you go through times when it seems like your dream and destiny are all but dead, do not fret. If God made a promise about you that promise is not changing . . . you are. By the time Joseph landed in his place of power and authority, he was not the same young man who had gotten on his brothers' nerves. The journey had changed him. He was a man who knew that the only way he had navigated the transitions of life was because God was in control . . . and God was good. Joseph had no desire to strut around with a big head. All he could do was give the Lord the glory. Joseph's situations did change, and thankfully, so did he.

Your situations can change . . . and so can you.

Transition can also imply a passage from one season to the next. This means that one door is closing and another one is opening. Transitions, no matter how painful, are what God uses to open up what is next in our lives. Without transitions, we get stuck and we remain in a place God is no longer committing himself to blessing. In Psalm 37, the psalmist David tells us the steps of a good man are ordered of the Lord. Steps speak of process and transition. Do not ask God to order your steps if you won't commit to moving your feet!

I believe you are reading this book because God wants to prepare you for what is next. Dreams you thought were buried and done in these times of transition are about to receive new life. The enemy has tried to convince you that you are stuck and there is no way you can rise to see your destiny fulfilled. However, this book is going to show you that, no matter what, it looks like it is not over.

Your transitions have been and are critical. The fact is, when God orders your steps, you don't just transition, you transition to position!

You and my friend Josh Carter are about to embark on a journey of hope together. Josh has done an incredible job of using the revelation of the burial season of Christ found in John 19:38-42 to unfold the steps and path to successfully navigate the transitions of life and ministry. Stepping into your destiny could be just a read away.

Even if your dream seems dead and buried, do not give up! God is not through. Anything he has said about you is coming to life! Get ready to discover the power of the process and promise of new beginnings as you dive into this great book, *Buried.*

Pastor Jim Raley
Lead Pastor
Calvary Christian Center

Introduction

I will never forget it. It was 2:34 a.m. and I had not slept a wink. The feeling in my stomach was not from pizza or a case of food poisoning, but rather from an inward feeling of conviction and intense stirring of God's Spirit. I had felt this before, but only in the monumental spiritual shifts in my life.

This was the same feeling I had felt on the side of the road when the Lord called me into full-time ministry. It was the same feeling I experienced the night before I took my position as the youth pastor at Farmington Heights Church in Wilson, which would become the "the9tenmovement." What could God want now?

My wife and I were comfortable. We were in a newly built facility, leading a thriving youth and young adult ministry with hundreds of students in attendance each week. Beyond that, we were traveling throughout the country, speaking at camps and conferences to thousands of people each year. We had the best of both worlds! However, truth be told, we did not have the best of God's plan. God was visiting me to call me again. What he would ask me next would change everything—literally change everything.

I got out of bed and kneeled. God's presence instantly overwhelmed me. I began to weep uncontrollably. I remember crying out, asking, "What do you want?"

Though accustomed to my late night prayer sessions, my wife woke up as I prayed. She sensed this was different. She did not speak, but lay silently—a spectator watching the encounter unfold.

As tears rolled down my face, the voice of the Lord cut through the room and echoed loudly in my spirit. It was a booming, yet gentle voice that spoke with clarity and urgency. My heart was vulnerable, and my ears were open. This is what I heard:

Josh, I am calling you to be my evangelist. I have been calling you. I need your obedience and full participation. Tonight, I am calling you for the last time. For the places I want to take you will require your full focus. I need you to trust me, I need your yes.

Before my flesh could fully digest what God had said, my spirit man responded with a resounding, "Yes, Lord." I began to weep again. My wife joined me, weeping and praying for me.

As we dried the tears, I shared with her what God had said and wanted. She was in complete agreement. The time had come to transition into the world of full-time evangelism. My yes to God was the start of a process that would lead me step by step into the waters I now swim in as a full-time evangelist. In the days to follow, God handed me a second assignment. You are holding it right now.

One thing I did not tell you in the story above is that God had already been dealing with us about moving into full-time evangelism. However, every time God began to prompt me, I would respond with terrible excuses: "Lord, I'm already doing it," or "I can do both—youth pastor and evangelize." Even up to a year previous to the encounter I described above, this kind of dialogue was just about a daily fight between God and I—an ongoing battle of wills.

One thing I had agreed with God to do was write a book. In asking God what to write about, he took me to an Easter sermon I had preached in 2012 called "Buried." The crux of the sermon dealt with handling transitions in life (sound familiar?). I had become excited and anxious to dive into this process of writing, but steadily hit writing blocks and could never find enough time to really sit down and write.

However, after that 2:34 a.m. encounter, my passion to write was resurrected and I understood why I had not been able to write this book yet. God was not going to allow me to write about a topic I understood from a biblical standpoint, but had not personally experienced.

Over the past year, the book you hold has written itself, through experiences, study, and revelation. It is my prayer that you will be more than encouraged. I have asked God to allow my experience to become your wisdom in dealing with the transitions of life.

This book was written for anyone dealing with any kind of transition. Whether you are going through or facing basic life transitions, relationship transitions, or even ministry transitions, this book will speak to every part of the journey and help you navigate.

As you read, you will find a biblical account that will ultimately become your road map on the highway called transition. Use it. Apply the principles. Take your time with it. If taken to heart, I promise you that what you will read on the pages to come will bring understanding and blessing. When you finish this book, you will be able to identify the specific stops on the road of transition. You'll know where you are and how to help someone else identify where they are. You will be able to navigate transition no matter the type of transition it is. I promise, this book will not bless you because of its author or my personal experience, but because of the added blessing of God's Word and God's voice.

Now, take the journey . . . your destiny awaits.

Chapter 1

Transition: What Is It All About?

I am getting old. Yes, to some I am just a young guy. However, as I enter my thirties, I am already coming to the startling revelation that, quite frankly, is causing me to panic a bit. I bet you are wondering what kind of revelation could cause a young, vibrant, hardworking man to have bouts of panic and anxiety. It is almost embarrassing to admit, but the one thought that seems to be wrecking my mind lately is that life is *full* of transitions.

It is as simple as this: Transition is unavoidable for anything that is alive and moving, inevitable for any person going somewhere with their life, and completely necessary to fulfill one's purpose and destiny.

No, you have not picked up the wrong book. Rest assured, this book is for you. However, before you put it down, throw it away, or even give it away, take a second to come to grips with the notion that *life is all about transition*. In our daily lives, we face transition on a consistent basis. We face transition in our jobs, relationships, and family dynamics.

"Transition is unavoidable for anything that is alive and moving, inevitable for any person going somewhere with their life, and completely necessary to fulfill one's purpose and destiny."

No doubt by now you have already become conscious of the moving parts of transition in your own life. You are conscious of how different you look, sound, or feel compared to last week, month, or year. You are conscious of the style differences from past seasons of your life. You are conscious of how your relationships, friendships, and fellowships have rearranged themselves. You are also conscious of how far you have really come, and the fact that while you may not be where you want to be, you are indeed on your way.

It Is Kind of Like . . .

If I were to liken transition to anything, it would be to a roller coaster. If you are a roller coaster person, you just got super excited. However, I must make a quick confession: *I am not you!* Roller coasters are the devil. To me, there is no worse feeling than having your jaw pushed against your face, creating the ever so attractive quadruple chin look. (Do you sense the sarcasm?) As much as I despise roller coasters, there is a valuable illustration in them of the transitions of life.

The Line

The entire roller coaster experience screams transition. First, there is the line—the long line that seems to awaken and heighten your expectation. (I must insert a key thought here: *Your expectation determines your experience!*) It is not so much that you wait, but rather how you wait that determines what you receive from the experience. This is why Isaiah, the eagle eye prophet said, "But those who *wait* upon the Lord shall renew *their* strength; (Isaiah 40:31). The twenty-twenty farsighted prophet is communicating that flying takes strength and movement takes muscle. Most people will never need to be taught to wait, but at some point in time, almost every person will need to be taught *how* to wait. The solution to the wait is the renewing of one's strength. The wait is an opportunity to make sure your strength is where it needs to be to handle the flight to the destination. While you are waiting you ought to be gaining strength, building faith, and developing your gifts and God-given abilities, because at some point in time, the wait will be over and your moment will have arrived. The real question is, will you be ready?

The Seating

After the line comes the process of seating—or as I like to call it, the positioning. Trust me: Positioning matters. The proper position is necessary for a sufficient start on the roller coaster. Without this, you would lack the momentum to carry you through those lovely corkscrews and figure eights. This would leave you in a dangerous place (even dead). It is virtually the same in your walk with God.

God will position you to start correctly because, with God, there are two distinct principles that come with proper positioning. First, whatever God starts, he sustains. If God authors it, more than authorizing the journey, he is assuming responsibility for whatever comes along the way. So the key question to ask before starting any journey—whether in dating, marriage, job, or friendships—is, "Did God really start it?" Second, he who has begun a good work in us is faithful to complete it (Philippians 1:6).

God has no interest in leaving us halfway to our destiny. He has assured us our promised destination if we will not quit in the journey. It is the hope of God's help that continues to keep us moving forward even when the terrain of our purpose does not match what God originally said about the finish line. However, at the end of the day, the main reason God is into starting right is because he knows it is nearly impossible for us to finish right if we do not start right. Once again I reiterate: Positioning matters.

Starting is hard! However, starting is the prerequisite for finishing. Still, the intimidating view of a new start can keep us from starting at all. All my life I have heard people say, "It is not how you start, it is how you finish that matters." This is only a partial truth. The whole truth is that we need a successful start. If we do not start right, we will not finish right. This is why God specializes in *new starts!* He will interrupt a life going in the wrong direction and give an individual a fresh start. Why? So that the new start can bring them to their destined end.

The seating is a picture of your new position for a new start. Purpose in your heart and mind that *you must start—you have to start!* Know that if you start you cannot and will not be stopped!

Now, before you get too comfortable in your seat and the heavy breathing stops, you are interrupted by the jolt of the gears and the car lurches forward. You begin what I call the "ride up." This ascent is beautiful and somewhat soothing compared to the nerve-racking period you just endured as you waited in line. You laugh out loud with your neighbor and enjoy the view.

The View

The view. Did I mention the view? It is beautiful, breathtaking, and often awe-inspiring! The view gives more than a new perspective; it gives us a deeper understanding of the past behind us and a hint of the future ahead of us. Thank God for glimpses of understanding. It is in these places that we pause for a moment in the journey and say: "Now I get it," or, "That makes sense now." I have learned that we appreciate God's omniscience when we are strapped in and taken to higher places. It is here that we gain divine perspective. After all, his ways and thoughts are *higher* than ours. When we are caught up in this perspective, we not only come to appreciate and love God more deeply, we become increasingly thankful for his perfect plan and sovereign will for our lives as well.

The up parts of life are amazing. In these places, life seems effortless and wonderful. It is here that the stresses of any of the previous experiences seem to melt away and we are ushered into greater perspective and joy. Everyone loves the ups. Very rarely do you hear a complaint from someone after they gain better clarity and perspective. No one grumbles about promotions and elevation. It is all smiles in seasons of getting a better paying job, or having drama free relationships or friendships.

Now, we should enjoy the ups of life. Breathe them in with the people you love. Use them as opportunities to praise God and bless others as an example of what God can do with a surrendered, submitted life.

I have learned that most of the time, God gives us ups to minister to someone else's downs. How are you using your ups? Are you using them to minister faith and hope? Are you using them to be a source of encouragement and motivation to someone else who is waiting in line for an up moment in life?

"God gives us ups to minister to someone else's downs."

At the pinnacle of your up is a moment—a moment of achievement, accomplishment, and arrival. It feels good to be on top. It is incredible to live and view life from the mountaintop. However, there is always more to a moment when it comes to your movement with God. God uses moments to breed *momentum.*

Moments are designed to propel us to the proverbial "next thing in God." They help us move away from our past life and into abundant life. Maximize the moments in your destiny by letting momentum thrust you into purpose as an unstoppable force on an unstoppable course.

"God uses moments to breed *momentum*."

The Drop

I wish I could stop here. I wish I could say that the journey ends with the ups, and that you will live the rest of your life in a constant ascent into greatness with no trouble or transition. Unfortunately, this would be a lie. Honestly, all of the previous thoughts I have shared—the line, seating and view—were *not* why I was prompted by the Holy Spirit to write this book. What you have read to this point are all of the pleasantries of the ride called "destiny and purpose."

I wish I could skip the remainder of the book and tell you that life is all ups and that the wait is always short, the view always incredible, and that you can live in those moments forever. However, again, this would be a lie—a bold-faced lie. I have written the remainder of this book on a subject no one likes to discuss—specifically the moments about which no one told me or preached to me. To what moments am I referring? I am referring to the moments *after* the highs of life, between the great times, when the true *transitions of life* occur.

With the roller coaster there is an aching feeling that the drop is imminent. In life, we experience these drop moments when we get those heartbreaking phone calls, disappointing letters, or hear devastating news. It is the place between the pinnacles. Life is full of these crazy, chaotic moments.

When these moments hit, remember that the drops they bring—as horrifying and scary as they are—are still part of the ride. The drop moments and up moments coordinate, serving as vehicles to bring you to the destination to which God has called you.

The Bible speaks to this in Romans 8:28 when it declares: "And we know that *all* things work together for good to those who love God, to those who are the *called* according to his *purpose*." Did you catch that?

All things, good and bad, are working together. You need both for a successful journey to destiny.

What Is It All About?

This book is designed to help you navigate the transitions of life. I asked God where I could find the best illustration of this for you, from the Bible. I thought for sure I would find it in the Old Testament in the life stories of men like Joseph or David, which scream transition. Then I thought God might point me to the well-traveled, adventurous life of the great apostle Paul, but the Lord did not take me there. Instead, he took me to a passage of scripture in the Gospel of John, sandwiched between some of the greatest scriptures ever penned. It is here, in John 19:38-42, that God brought to my attention the burial of his Son Jesus; a three-day season of transition called burial, right there between his gruesome sacrificial death on the cross and his glorious, sudden resurrection. As I read it, I was struck by what could arguably be considered the greatest transition season of all time.

I will use hidden gems from this passage as the infrastructure for learning how to handle the transitions of life. Armed with these truths, you will answer tough, introspective questions like these: How am I handling the transitions of life? What do I do when everything around me changes?

My hope is that the wisdom and revelation in this book will inspire you and reveal God's perfect plan for you, even if you are in the midst of isolation and devastation in your transition. Remember, transition is momentary yet necessary. When it is finished, you will come out better than ever for it; ready to walk in every new thing God has prepared for you.

Before reading each chapter, I encourage you to read the key passage again, John 19:38-42. As you read each chapter, take notes. Take inventory. Constantly place the road markers of this book around your life experiences, and track your transition through every chapter.

We need to get a move on. You have somewhere to be!

Chapter 2

After This: The Birthplace of Transition

I could not believe my eyes. There was no way what I was seeing was really happening. It was the morning of September 11, 2001 (9/11). At the time, I was a high school senior who had stayed home sick that day. When I awoke and turned on the TV, I saw the smoke pouring out of the twin towers in New York City and the ensuing chaos, just 250 miles north of us. As a resident of Hagerstown, Maryland, I found myself close to the center of the action on that heartbreaking, historical day. Nearly one hundred miles to our west, terrorists crashed United flight 93 in Shanksville, Pennsylvania. Approximately seventy-five miles to our east, they slammed another jetliner into the Pentagon. I felt helpless.

Every fifteen to thirty minutes, our house would shake as F-16s flew low overhead—just above our rooftops, it seemed. As the towers fell and the chaos continued, I found myself caught up in one specific thought I even asked my parents as the day faded into night: "What will happen next?" I was consumed—not with the tragedy—but with the response.

Over the days that followed, I watched the coverage of thousands of workers searching for survivors, bodies, and doing their best to clear the rubble of what had been the World Trade Center. The actions of those workers and the patriotic stance of our nation in the face of it brought my thought of what would happen next to a powerful crescendo. The lesson that was seared into my heart was that even after the worst of tragedies, we can begin again. I realized that what was yet to come was going to be better than what had come before. The tragedy of the attack was horrible, but after the dust settled, it created a moment for what I call an "after this."

You Need This . . . After This

Of all the ways to bring us into the moment of Christ's burial, God eloquently chose to breathe the words "after this" into John, the gospel writer. I was blown away at how two words spoke so profoundly to the genesis of transition.

For any transition to begin, you will need these two simple, yet powerful words. You will need an *after this*!

As God took me through the passage of scripture I am using as the key passage for this book, I could not get over those opening two words. There is no other way to say it than that the phrasing of the Holy Spirit had me completely mesmerized.

"For any transition to begin, you will need these two simple, yet powerful words. You will need an *after this*!"

The truth is, *after this* is the prerequisite for transition to begin. God often uses *after this* moments because it is impossible for him to bring us into the new and next if we are content and comfortable with what already is. Our love of comfort often keeps the Holy Spirit (the comforter), from being active and supernatural in our destiny. We are usually just one nerve-racking, life-altering, uncomfortable step away from seeing God do the miraculous in our lives. In other words, our comfort is a destiny constrictor. It will constrict us from moving into God's purpose and plan, and it will constrict the Holy Spirit from doing the *super* part of the supernatural.

What I am about to tell you may make you uneasy or uncomfortable, but here goes. When God sees us being unresponsive to the challenges of life, he will permit adversity, trouble, or even tragedy to help bring the changes he so desires.

To illustrate what I mean, take a look at the newly birthed church in the book of Acts. In chapter 8 of that book, the New Testament church in Jerusalem is under intense persecution. You might be wondering what these men did so wrong to be so greatly afflicted, and more importantly, what errors they made to be left so unprotected during their time of persecution. After all, these men were full of the Holy Spirit, working incredible miracles, and doing amazing signs in Jerusalem under the banner of Christianity.

The answer in Acts 8 seems to be elusive until we place our current location against Christ's Great Commission. According to Jesus, Jerusalem was to be a starting point for the gospel (Acts 1:8). It was to be a starting place and base for the good news to go into all the world.

What happened in Jerusalem in the beginning was powerful. It included luminary events like the upper room, the gift of baptism of the Holy Spirit, three thousand people giving their lives to Christ on the Day of Pentecost, the lame being healed, and the church growing at a furious pace.

However, in the midst of all the good that had happened to the disciples and the church in Jerusalem, Christ's call was larger than just Jerusalem. It was a call to reach Judea, Samaria, and ultimately, the ends of the earth. After this extended period of time, they were still in Jerusalem and had yet to even touch the next level of the Great Commission.

If I had to title Acts 8, I would make it simple, maybe even a little too direct, and possibly a little rude and unbiblical. I would say that in Acts 8, God stirred up a stuck church. On the surface, led by anointed men, the newly established church was under persecution and in utter chaos. However, upon further review, one can see that God —who is not the author of confusion—is allowing and using the chaos to stir up a stuck group of disciples to see that there was more than where they were.

As long as you are breathing and living, there is always more. God will bring finality to one thing to begin the next. It is on the heels of one of these seasons that you will find your *after this*.

I wonder what is coming to an end for you. I am curious as to what situation God is using or has used (no matter how painful or chaotic) to bring you into the genesis of your transition to mutter, "After this." If you have found yourself saying, "After this," from a biblical standpoint, it is obvious your transition has begun.

So What Is the Definition?

So what is an *after this*? How do we define it? It is important that your *after this* is definable. The goal in defining your *after this* is not to conjure up hurtful memories and painful past experiences, but to see what God has done and, ultimately, where God is trying to take you.

This is my—I stress *my*—definition of *after this*: "A phrase that bridges and breaks two different, yet connected experiences. It gives context to the upcoming attraction based upon a previous showing." *After this* can be a beautiful or devastating experience (or *both!*). For example, for a person experiencing the tragedy of a hurricane, *after this* can hold a sigh of relief from the passing storm, but give way to feelings of sheer heartache and emotional distress as a result of the devastation of the storm.

What is your *after this*? What result has your most recent *after this* brought to your life? Truth be told, every passing decision brings us into an experience resulting in an *after this*.

It Is Up to You

Decisions are the mind's breaths. Consciously and unconsciously, we make hundreds of decisions in our daily lives. We inhale a thought and exhale an action, culminating in a decision.

Most decisions require little to no thought. Decisions like brushing your teeth, taking a shower, and choosing your outfit do not bring a sweat to your brow, nor do they drastically alter the landscape of your life. However, some decisions do. We know long before we ever make them that they will greatly affect us and those around us. We know that some decisions will change the trajectory of our lives, either slowing us down or putting us on the fast track to destiny. These decisions are painstaking.

With every decision we make, we flesh out and bring into the world of experience the thoughts that merely existed in our minds. The aftermath of the experience brings us into a consequence—positive or negative—called an *after this*.

> "With every decision we make, we flesh out and bring into the world of experience the thoughts that merely existed in our minds."

Jesus was not without the same kind of decisions. After all, he was sent to earth to save and restore humanity to its proper position and relationship with God. The Bible is clear that Jesus was tempted in all things (Hebrews 4:15), yet remained sinless. This means that Jesus had to make conscious daily decisions that affected his everyday life as well as his overall mission and purpose.

The Bible clearly shows us that Jesus made all the right choices, but not without perfect help. It was with the help of the Holy Spirit that Jesus made decisions that led him to fulfill his purpose. Who is helping your decision making? Which voices are responsible for your latest and greatest decision? Is the Holy Spirit leading these voices? At the end of the day, before we take any advice from others, our decisions should be shaped by the Word of God and the helping of the Holy Spirit.

The toughest decision Jesus had to make was not one of whether to show compassion or love. He never had to reason or battle within himself on whether or not to heal someone, or whether or not to respond to those in need. He made his life-altering decision in the Garden of Gethsemane when, through a blood drenched brow, he began to catch the most vivid of glimpses of the cross that lay before him. He confirmed this decision through the statement, "Father, if it is Your will, take this cup away from me; nevertheless not My will, but Yours, be done" (Luke 22:42) The yes of Jesus would ultimately bring him into the experience of the cross.

Just Like Jesus

In most cases, we are privy to the public consequences of Jesus's yes. We see through the eyes of the writers of the Gospels his horrific and painful death. They paint a vivid picture of its severity, detailing that our Lord was beaten and bruised, spit upon and mocked, tied to a whipping post and left with 39 stripes upon his back from a cat-o'-nine-tails. Jesus was weighed down with a wooden cross on his back, wore a real crown of thorns on his head, and had his hands and feet pierced with real nails. Just as we recoil in horror as we look upon the suffering servant of which the prophet Isaiah spoke, we see a real Jesus hanging on that cross and gasping for every breath. In that moment, the full weight of the world's sin, rejection from the father, and the burden of salvation crushed him. With one last breath, and with all the strength he had left, Jesus shouted the most infamous, life-giving words . . . *"It is finished!"* (John 19:30)

This is where we begin our journey. We begin here because this is where Jesus began his *after this*. Most of us are acquainted with the suffering and pain of life. However, when it is all said and done, the cross most accurately speaks to moments of doing what God has said (obedience) even while in excruciating pain or complete confusion.

We know what it is like to say yes to God and his plan with our whole hearts, and then seemingly walking right into heartbreak. However, the pain has a purpose, the rejection a resolve. We need it and the suffering it brings. Without it, there really could be no *after this*.

How does creation come out of our chaos? How does Job get double without trouble? How does Joseph get a palace without a pit, Potiphar's house, and a prison? The list of real-life examples from the Bible could go on and on.

My point is; God is the author and finisher of our faith (Hebrews 12:2). He is the God whose thoughts are above our thoughts, and his ways are above our ways (Isaiah 55:9). He is a God who orders our steps (Psalms 37:23) and works *all* things for our good (Romans 8:28). I am saying that whether it is the valley of the shadow of death or the belly of a whale, the backdrop of bad is oftentimes the greatest setup for an *after this*!

As you look back over your life and pinpoint your *after this* moments, I encourage you to embrace a new perspective: If you are still standing after weathering the storm, rejoice! If you have breath in your lungs, praise God! If you survived the hurtful things people said and did, be thankful! Why? All of this has positioned you for an *after this*. Whenever you have an *after this*, it will not be long before God shows you its purpose was larger then the momentary pain.

If you have survived the *after this*, a moment of glory is on your horizon and a divine understanding is around the corner. When all is said and done, God is going to give you clarity, revealing the real purpose behind it and where you are in your destiny.

Chapter 3

Accomplished: What "After This" Did for Your Transition

Joseph Kagarama. It is likely you are unfamiliar with this name, but for me, it is a name I will never forget. I met this incredible man on a ministry trip to Uganda to preach at the East Africa Church of God youth convention in 2014. Little did I know that this man, the presiding overseer of the Church of God in East Africa, would leave a lifelong imprint on my life and ministry.

Bishop Kagarama is not a man of many words, but when he does speak, he does so with wisdom and power. I very distinctly remember first meeting him. As we pulled into the compound where the youth convention was held, I could feel the presence of God tangibly. It nearly overwhelmed me. As Bishop Kagarama welcomed us in, even as he shook my hand I could sense he had been with God. During the praise and worship, I saw him place both hands against one of the walls while praying fervently. He then took the platform and elegantly welcomed the people.

As he spoke, every person in the place was captivated by his words, though he said very few. He welcomed me to the pulpit and sat quietly as I ministered. Every once in a while, I heard a gentle amen come from his direction.

As the sessions ran into the lunch hour, we stopped just long enough to eat the meal prepared by his incredibly hospitable team. After receiving the food, we returned to our seats. My seat was right next to Bishop Kagarama. Though I had preached all morning, as we sat to eat I had no idea that the real ministry was about to begin. What I was about to hear from this servant of God would echo in my ears and burn in my spirit.

It all started with one simple question. I asked, "How long have you been in ministry?" He did not answer me with a simple number. Instead, he answered me in a narrative of experiences. He spoke to me of the days of living under the harsh rule of the third Ugandan president, Idi Amin. His stories had me mesmerized. I could not eat my lunch, I was so captivated by the words Bishop Kagarama spoke.

Nearly every story was epic in proportion. He recounted once being in mid-sermon when Ugandan authorities arrested him and his brothers for preaching the gospel. They were cuffed and pushed into a van to be transported to a hellish prison or worse. At one point, the brothers began to pray in the Spirit. Suddenly, those who arrested them began to argue with one another so intensely that eventually, in frustration, they released their captives. As Bishop Kagarama shared this, I remember thinking to myself, *This is more than a great story; this is what the book of Acts must have looked and sounded like in real life.*

As he told his stories, tears began to well up in his eyes. I could not help but feel the same emotions as this man felt. As we both wiped the tears from our faces, I was gripped by the man's unrelenting commitment and sacrifice for the gospel. He had paid a tremendous price to advance a kingdom he so evidently believed in.

This conversation wrecked me. However, I misread what was happening. I thought his emotion was connected to his past experiences. I was wrong. I realized this fully when he looked me squarely in the eyes and said, "It was all worth it." As he smiled at several young people walking past the table, I got it. Bishop Kagarama's suffering and sacrifice were never about him. Those tears were not connected to his *pain*. They were tears of *joy* for what his sacrifice had given way too.

As lunch ended, the bishop made one last comment to me. Honestly, this statement is what birthed the heartbeat of this chapter. With a smile, the bishop said, "Watching these young people worship God freely, and hearing them go after God withe their whole hearts is my reward, my legacy."

Bishop Joseph Kagarama understood something I had not. He understood that our pain and suffering have more than a purpose; they have a mission to accomplish, a goal to complete. He understood that if

we hang on long enough, the sky will clear and the pain will subside. If we can let go of the horrible part of the experience, we will be privy to a greater perspective on the accomplishments of our *after this*.

Let It Go, Let It Go

Move on! Get over it! Get past it! Build a bridge! I am sure you have heard one of these clichés before from at least one well-intentioned person in your life, whether someone close to you or someone you barely knew. Perhaps someone said one of these to you in a way that was not well intended or caring. No matter the intention or level of care shown by the speaker, these phrases are hard to swallow, even on our way out of the horrible circumstances that elicited them.

It is often hard to let go of the pain of yesterday. We tend to hold on to our history without understanding that it is keeping us from our destiny.

Why is it so hard to move forward? Why are we so often content to remain the victim and not walk in victory? Why can we not place ourselves on the other side of our *after this*? I know each of those questions alone could become another book, but I want to hint at what I think is the biggest reason we stay stuck: We need a resolution.

Moving forward is hard when there is no closure or validation to why we went through what we did. It is often easier for us to make progress when the purpose of our past pain is revealed to us. In other words, we can go because we know! You can see the accomplishments of what you have been through with the lenses of twenty-twenty hindsight.

"It is often easier for us to make progress when the purpose of our past pain is revealed to us."

If we truly believe that everything has a purpose, then we must believe that everything that happens in our lives is to accomplish something. Every purpose has a purposeful end; a place where its glory is seen and the manifestation of what it was called to do comes to pass.

If our pain is purposeful, its success is found in what is accomplished through it. Fortunately for us, the accomplishments of our pai

and tragedies is not gauged by how much they hurt us, but by how much they changed us for the good.

Have you ever asked, "Why?" Regardless of your answer, one of the benefits of your *after this* (see the previous chapter) is an awareness of the accomplishments of your season of suffering. God wastes nothing. No, you heard me right: God uses everything in every season. In fact, it is never about *what left* in tough seasons, it is about *what is left* in those seasons.

Widows and Prophets

Proof of this can be found in the Old Testament, in the book of Second Kings, chapter four. This chapter contains an account of a widow woman whose life is under an extreme amount of stress. The conditions and circumstances she is enduring are nothing short of horrendous. There is a famine in the land, her husband is deceased, and she has *no* money! To make matters worse, creditors have come to collect on the family's debt. If she cannot pay, her sons will be taken as payment. I cannot imagine the peril, the suffering, and the heartache of this woman who has lost so much and is days away from losing it all.

In the middle of this woman's tragic story, help comes in the form of the prophet Elisha. His first words of help upon arrival at the widow's home are fascinating. The Bible records that Elisha asks the widow, "What do you have in the house?" This poor woman must have thought, *I am doomed! If the help I am looking for is coming from my house, then we should just pack it in and give up.*

Her response is deafening. In 2 Kings 4:2, the widow declares, "Your maidservant has *nothing* in the house *but* a jar of oil" (emphasis added). This woman had no idea that oftentimes, what is left has more power in it than what left. She did not realize that small things in our eyes become large in the hand of God. Out of obedience, the widow took what remained of the oil and set below the jar of oil the borrowed vessels she was commanded to get. The moment of truth came when she poured what remained, and what remained was multiplied to meet her need (and then some). It was only when she ran out of vessels that the oil ceased. What a miracle! God supernaturally met her need out of what remained, and he can do the same for you.

Take a moment to take inventory in your life of what remains. No matter how small it is, when God is in it, he can take your not enough and turn it into more than enough.

"This woman had no idea that oftentimes, what is left has more power in it than what left. She did not realize that small things in our eyes become large in the hand of God."

I am telling you that God is not finished with you. The "seasons of crucifixion" may crush us and even seemingly "kill" us, but they do not strip us of the accomplishments that our troubles have produced or future glory we will possess.

Jesus and His "After This" Accomplishments

What about Jesus? What about his *after this*? John 19:38 is clear that Jesus had an *after this*. His season of suffering—his torture and crucifixion—could easily have warranted the greatest pity party the world had ever seen. He had every right to complain, gripe, or even be disgruntled with what he had to go through. However, this was not his mind-set. Beyond the gospels, the New Testament proclaims: "For the joy that was set before Him endured the cross" (Hebrews 12:2).

Jesus understood what we often do not: There is an *after this*. He understood that God would use that season and his purpose would accomplish things greater than his own mind could conceive.

It is necessary theologically to list out these accomplishments to see that there is more happening in crucifixion seasons than can be seen by the naked eye. The list of crucifixion accomplishments can be lengthy, but here are six I believe to be the most important, the six that speak at the highest volume, for undoubtedly, Christ's death was all these things.

1. The Greatest Moment in History
This one moment broke history in half. It is out of the crucifixion of Christ that time was divided into BC (before Christ) and AD (after death). The cross now stands as the symbol not just of our good news, but the day when who we used to be ended and who we were intended to be began.

2.   *The Crux of Christianity*

The cross of Christ's crucifixion is the crux of Christianity. It is the height of our freedom. The cross and Christ's crucifixion speak to the world of our beliefs and doctrine. His death high on the hill of Golgotha are the pinnacle of our belief: "For God so loved the world that He gave His only begotten Son, that whoever believes in Him should not perish but have everlasting life" (John 3:16).

3.   *The Moment of Redemption*

Perhaps the most miraculous moment for the world was when this bleeding Jesus, in that moment, redeemed us from the cold grasp of sin and death. Taking up the cross symbolized Christ taking my sin (past, present, and future) and reconciling us to God. We are now redeemed and free by the precious blood of Jesus. Crucially, his blood was shed and not spilled, making his death sacrificial, not accidental. As Scripture declares, "Let the redeemed of the Lord *say so!*" (Psalm 107:2, KJV).

4.   *Where the Wrath of God Was Satisfied*

Christ's death made a way by which we could come to God. Our righteousness was, according to the Bible, as "filthy rags" (Isaiah 64:6). On our best day trying to be good people, we were still unable to reach the standard of a holy God. Christ's death gave us this righteousness and now we are able to boldly approach the throne of grace (Hebrews 4:16). Our access into the holy place was forever granted by the sent Son and a torn veil.

5.   *The Ultimate Sacrifice of Love*

The crucifixion of Christ brought Christ to his death. The Word of God declares that there is no greater love than this, that a man lay down his life for his friends (John 15:13). The crucifixion became the example of those very words. The sacrifice of love shattered the very definition of love. From that moment on, love would never be seen as a simple declaration but recognized at its highest level as a sacrificial demonstration.

6.   *A Substitutionary Death*

Finally, but by no means the least important, is the concept of Christ's crucifixion being substitutionary. It is gut-wrenching to know that truly, the cross was for me. Jesus the God-man came to earth and lived a sinless life, yet he became sin (2 Corinthians 5:21). What a breathtaking truth of love and grace, to know that by all rights, we needed to be crucified *like* Christ, but through his substitutionary death, we are now called to be crucified *with* Christ (Galatians 2:20).

Mission Accomplished?

Listing the accomplishments of Christ's crucifixion speaks volumes to our doctrine, theology, and view of God. However, the underlying theme is that God truly wastes nothing and certainly uses everything. He calls us according to his purpose and accomplishes his perfect plan even in the midst our discomfort and the most painful parts of our lives.

What has your crucifixion moment accomplished? What did the drama, divorce, breakup, death, or financial problem produce in you? More importantly, what will its accomplishments leave for someone else to see? How will it encourage them? I encourage you to take a look. I challenge you to write each crucifixion moment down, along with all of its accomplishments. As painful or tough as this may be, you must confront these crucifixion moments for the sake of gaining clarity of what they have positively produced in your life. If you choose to find and focus on the accomplishments, you will ultimately find your closure, come into understanding about all you have faced, and begin to confidently move forward.

In the end, do not lose heart. Refuse to be discouraged. Never believe the devil's lie that God hates you and that God is absent from you. Instead, embrace the seasons of affliction.

The apostle Paul called them "momentary afflictions" (2 Corinthians 4:17-18), and promised that these short moments were working for us a far more exceeding and eternal weight of glory. Let the pain produce the accomplishments. Let the tragedy turn to triumph. This momentary and temporary issue is accomplishing something that is eternal and lasting.

What those around at the time did not know was that the few hours spent in crucifixion would change the landscape of time, eternity, and the spiritual well-being of all mankind. Be convinced: If it already worked for Christ's good, it will work for your good and his plan as well.

Chapter 4

Imitate This: Transition's First Step

Nothing, and I mean nothing, beats a great impersonation or imitation. I have been known to do a few really good ones myself. There is an art to taking who you are and letting someone else's mannerisms, voice tone, and inflection come through. I am sure you have heard some great (and probably not so good) impersonations. Undoubtedly, you know someone who thinks they are great at imitations or impersonations, who should probably just stick to his or her day job.

No matter what you have heard or seen concerning imitation or impersonation, the fact of the matter is that it is a part of the call of believers. Paul clearly communicated this to us in his letter to the church at Ephesus when he urged them to be "imitators of God as dear children" (Ephesians 5:1). This call for imitation is not a mere suggestion to us, it is a sincere command of God; a part of our *new life* and *new nature*!

The previous chapters have spoken to the pains of life and the trauma found in seasons of suffering. They have flipped the light on to reveal the depth of God's power in those seasons. They have shown how Christ, our example, has shown us a blueprint for stepping into the destiny and ultimate purpose of God for our lives. They have shown us the vital ground on which transition is initiated. They liberated us to move into what God has waiting for us.

Transitions First Step

You may be wondering how all of this fits into the transitions of life. I will answer that right now. I have found that while the pains of life unify us, they are not to be the thing that identifies us. Transition may need the "yesterday you" to begin, but it will need the "future you" to continue. God is eager to do more than remove your pain and suffering. He wants to reveal why you went through it. He is eager to shift your thinking and renew your mind, beginning with having you take on a new identity—an identity settled and secure in him, shaped and connected to your new expected end; not your former end. God promises you hope and a future (Jeremiah 29:11) that is connected to his plan, and the real you.

"Transition may need the 'yesterday you' to begin, but it will need the 'future you' to continue."

The first true step of transition is a shift in your identity. It involves navigating through the waters of a fresh start without remaining enamored with the old you. It is grabbing on to your new identity that breaks your feet free from the land of yesterday. When your pain is detached and distanced from your new identity, its power is no longer personal.

Let that sink in. In this place of transition, our personal pain is not really personal at all. It is where we find common ground with one another. Our pain is the lowest common denominator for making life connections and building solid friendships. When pain is no longer personal, it ushers us into a place that allows us to look past color, creed, and economic and social status. Pain is the equalizer, the starting line for purpose, and the initiator of transition.

What I am saying is simple: The fact that you have survived the crucifixion speaks to the fact that you are ready for the next step of transition. It is a step that brings you to the *new you* that is designed for your *next thing*. This step is called imitation.

Is It Bible?

For those of us who have found new life in Christ Jesus, our call is to become imitators of Christ. This is how we begin the metamorphosis that will ultimately move us into our expected end. The book of Romans shouts at us to present our bodies as a living sacrifice, holy and acceptable, unto God (Romans 12:1). It then proceeds to declare the how to the what by saying, "And do not be conformed to this world, but be transformed by the renewing of your mind" (Romans 12:2).

What a revelation! We become who God wants us to be by transforming ourselves through the doorway of a change of mind. However, this is not just any mind we are being asked to have or be renewed into. In Philippians 2:5-8 we read: "Let this mind be in you which was also in Christ Jesus, who, being in the form of God, did not consider it robbery to be equal with God, but made Himself of no reputation, taking the form of a bondservant, and coming in the likeness of men. And being found in appearance as a man, He humbled Himself and became obedient to the point of death, even the death of the cross."

"The first true step of transition is a shift in your identity. It involves navigating through the waters of a fresh start without remaining enamored with the old you."

The new mind and mind-set is the very mind of Christ. This is where we start to move forward despite all the seasons of pain, suffering, and even defeat. What mind or mind-set have you taken? Are you still in doubt? Have you quit? Are you trying to do the next thing with an old mind-set? If you answered yes to any of these questions, you are setting yourself up for a life of frustration instead of the abundant life Christ promised us (John 10:10). Grab your new mind! With it you will not only find a true transformation, you will properly begin the next step in your transition.

Imitation 101

After you have digested all you previously stated, the question is, what does real imitation look like (no pun intended)? If imitation of Christ is crucial to navigating the transitions of life, to what do we boil it down? Looking at the world of theater gives the best answer.

"To be or not to be . . . that is the question!" Sorry I just had to do that. I am *not* an actor. I have had no formal training in theater. However, I can say that I have always had a knack for doing impressions. Anyone who knows me would agree. Boiling down a great impersonation or imitation comes down to *four* elements: 1.Identifying the person to imitate; 2. Saying what they say; 3. Saying it how they say it, and; 4. Doing what they do (behavior) so that that what they do goes along with what they say.

Identifying the Person to Imitate

First things first: Before you pursue the rest of the steps mentioned above, you *must* accurately identify the person to imitate. Failing to do so might well create a false representation of the person you seek to imitate. Imitation is never based on your opinion of who you think the person is; it must be a sincere reflection of the truth of who the person truly is. This truth lends itself to a second principle: When pursuing an accurate imitation, you cannot pick or choose what you like or do not like.

It is the same with our call to imitate Christ. We must identify with all of who he is and what he has endured. We cannot remove from our imitation the uncomfortable parts of his life and the difficult things he encountered simply to feel comfortable. Doing so would be a poor representation and would rob others of understanding the very person of Christ.

Paul was clear on this in Ephesians when he wrote that we must be *imitators of Christ;* that is it, nothing more, nothing less, and certainty no one else but Christ. Basing our imitation on religion, tradition, second-hand relationship, or even church will not be effective in our imitation of Christ. It will only give us the watered down, overly opinionated imitation of our God-made flesh (John 1:14).

What this leads us to is this: Each of us *must* have a relationship with Christ ourselves. There is no better source of imitation than the intimacy gained through a personal relationship. This can be no truer than in our personal relationship with Christ. To be like him and become the best us, we must find intimacy with him. In so doing we will soon gain a relationship produced at the cross and developed through prayer and the reading of God's Word.

Saying What They Say

To imitate Christ is to be acquainted with God's Word. In the God-breathed pages of the Bible we capture the details of the life of God's only begotten Son. We find his voice in letters of red, speaking parables, teaching the twelve disciples, taking dominion over raging seas, and gently speaking to the distressed and hopeless.

This is where we begin. We must have Christ's words in our mouths. We must speak the things he spoke. We must become students of the Bible, dissecting his monologues towards God and his dialogues with people. We must bury the statutes of God in our hearts so that we can properly communicate them to the world we live in.

If his words will ever be in our mouths, then our eyes must be ever on his Word. God himself spoke to the weeping prophet, Jeremiah, in his prophetic infancy and declared, "Behold I have put my words in your mouth" (Jeremiah 1:9). My prayer is that I speak God's Word . . . that I talk like Jesus.

Saying It How They Say It

The third element of imitation is to go beyond being a vessel containing the words of God to release them in a life-giving, life-altering way. Tone is everything. My mother used to say "It's not what you say, it's how you say it." This is so important for believers in Christ to practice. The tone Christ used when he spoke ushered in his divine authority for the oppressed, released hope for the downtrodden, and paved the way for love from the Father.

We must be conscious of the same. How we speak is crucial. The Bible tells us that life and death are in the power of the tongue (Proverbs 18:21). It also declares that we ought to speak the truth in love (Ephesians 4:15). Every word we speak should not only carry the content of Christ, but be characterized by the attributes of Christ.

Doing What They Do

It has often been said that actions speak louder than words, and this is completely true. However, I would like to offer the idea that words speak louder *with* actions.

There is something powerful that happens when there is true alignment between what we say and what we do. Truth emerges. When this alignment happens, we extinguish confusion and eliminate the contradictions in all of our interactions. We give people a reason to believe, a reason to trust again. When this fails to happen, we limit our impact because we have lessened and devalued who we are and whom we are imitating.

People have a hard time following a contradiction. The reality of the matter is, it is hard for God to move us to where he is calling us when our words and deeds are not consistent. Set a goal that resolves that all you say and do will be in unity so that Christ will be exalted and your destiny completed.

"When your identity is set and your mind is renewed, it is only a matter of time before your feet begin to move in the direction of your true calling."

Transition starts with a transformation where our identity is changed and we are eternally altered due to our burning commitment to imitate Jesus. When your identity is set and your mind is renewed, it is only a matter of time before your feet begin to move in the direction of your true calling. God is calling you to imitate his Son. By so doing, he knows you will find the real you. Start today. Be like Christ. Discover the person full of potential, predestined for greatness, and preoccupied with God-given purpose. There is nothing that this new you cannot do. Everything is possible from here on out. Mark this moment in your life. Label it as the day you discovered how to discover the real you. It is all the momentum you need to keep moving in the middle of your transition.

Chapter 5

I Need What? Transition Needs Trust

> After this, Joseph of Arimathea, being a disciple of Jesus,
> but secretly, for fear of the Jews, asked Pilate that he
> might take away the body of Jesus; and Pilate gave *him*
> permission. So he came and took the body of Jesus.
>
> (John 19:38)

In this book so far, transition has only been presented in the context of transformation. We have only taken a look at what has to be recognized and perceived to understand the fact that transition is happening or on the horizon. We have explored the indicators of transition and the first step that must be taken to begin the journey.

However, transition always has a turning point. This is the moment by which your destiny stops living in a *theoretical* "what was" or "what might be" and crosses over to a "right now" *reality*. This is what I call a "word made flesh" moment. The Gospel of John tells us: "In the beginning was the Word" (John 1:1). God, sticking with his original pattern (see Genesis 1:3), started what he wanted to start through what he spoke. However, by the time we get to John 1:14 there is a dramatic shift. His word becomes flesh. His thoughts become realities. It is in this sudden shift that what started as something thought in the mind of God becomes something said from the mouth of God, and ends up getting legs and begins to live amongst us as present truth.

God wants to do more than make you aware of his promises and purpose for life. He wants it to become a reality for you. He is eager for you to walk in everything he has prepared for you. This is the next step in transition. This is the moment when God, with your faith and trust, begins to show you that you are truly on the move and your destiny is no longer a daydream, but a soon coming reality to your life.

Reality Check

Our passage of scripture in John 19 is no different. It follows this exact pattern of theory to reality, and takes its own sudden turn from the *after this* to the here and now.

The last thought of Christ in our minds is him hanging lifelessly from the cross upon which he was crucified. All we have is what has been. All the things he had said and promised seemed to be nothing but empty words. We see a beaten and nail-pierced dead man whose professed destiny of being an overcomer and savior of mankind seemed like a distant reality.

However, as believers we truly begin to see the transformational stage of transition subside as the realistic side of transition emerges. This is the place where the *after this* moment has to give way to the next part in the incredible journey of transition called, "what's next"!

Get Real

I love my GPS. I use it for nearly every trip I take. Without it, I would be lost. (I am sorry for the cheesy joke.) My GPS was the source of a recent revelation. No matter where I am trying to go, the GPS will not and cannot take me there without first determining where I am. My point of origin, no matter where it may be, becomes my starting place to get to where I want to go. The GPS cannot make the mileage and estimated arrival known until the moment it discerns the reality of where I currently am.

God is no different. Our transparency with God seems to let him know that we are finally ready and need his help. It seems as if when we finally stop lying to ourselves, God's truth about who we are invades us and tells us what we are called to do, and ultimately, where we need to go next. The truth of our current location unlocks the vital information necessary for us to move forward.

The Bible is full of accounts of people who asked profound questions. However, the most profound question ever asked in the Bible did not come from man. It came from God. After Adam sinned, he hid himself. This remains our nature, to hide ourselves from God and the truth about us. As God approached the apex of his creation, he did not scold Adam or even become angry. He asked the most relevant question of his (and our) lives. Genesis 3:9 says that God, in the cool of the day, opened his mouth and said to Adam, "Where are you?" Wow. How profound.

"The truth of our current location unlocks the vital information necessary for us to move forward."

Why would God ask this question? After all, God is God. It is not as if God did not know where Adam was. The purpose of the question was to reveal to *Adam* where Adam was. God never asks us questions so that he can collect information on what he does not know. He asks the questions to provide a revelation or evaluation to us.

Some of the most profound, life-altering God moments in your life will not stem from what God says. They will be birthed from what God asks. The revelation will come when you finally realize that God is more than ready. He is merely waiting for you to *get real.*

Real Talk

The truth of the matter is that to get your *what's next,* you need to be realistic about your *right now.* Honestly, professing your current location is the only true way to receive the next instruction to move in the right direction. God does his best work in our lives when we are truly honest about where we are.

The truth of the matter is that to get your *what's next,* you need to be realistic about your *right now.*

Have you ever been so tired of one season in your life that all you could pray was, "Lord, what's next?" Have you ever looked out at the world around you and felt as if everyone was moving forward except you? This is the second part of the struggle. Unlike the first struggle mentioned in chapter three (recognizing why you went through what you went through), the second part of the struggle gives way to an anxiety that speaks negatively towards your future. It will say things like, *You will never get to what is next for your life.* This anxiety will make you ask questions like:

- Will I ever find my special someone?
- Have I wasted too much time?
- Is there really anything else for me to do with my life?

That last question can dominate our conversation with God when we are in transition. Why? Because as human beings we are prone to get antsy and anxious when it comes to the next thing God wants to do.

The Step between Steps

For transition to take its next step, we must understand that true transition takes trust. No need to read that again, I will repeat it: Transition takes trust at every stage and place (and a great amount at that!).

"... true transition takes trust."

Success in the kingdom of God always demands two major things from us: obedience and trust. In light of this chapter's emphasis I will focus on the great hinge of transition: trust! Trust is the transport of transition. It is the place where we find hope and solace even if nothing in our lives seems to be moving or changing.

Trust remains in our silence. It talks even when we have run out of words. Trust never demands an explanation or conversation. It speaks when no one is even talking.

Trust Me . . .

As believers we must understand that there will be seasons when God moves and speaks loudly. As he delivers us, it will seem boisterous. When we are healed, it will appear to be glamorous and often be accompanied by a great ruckus. However, on the other side of the noise there are seasons of silence. Never mistake God's silence for his severance or his separation. Never assume he is not moving and working just because you cannot see him moving and working.

God is constantly working. He is always on the clock. In fact, the Bible says that God is constantly working all things together for our good. He is a God who does not sleep or slumber, just so you can! The bottom line is that he is *faithful*! One of the most comforting scriptures to solidify this point shouts out from holy writ: "He who has begun a good work in you will complete it" (Philippians 1:6). This is incredible news. Unlike people, God never starts something without finishing it. No matter how stuck you feel or how ready you think you are, be cognizant that God not only holds your purpose intact, he holds up the timing of that purpose in his perfect sovereignty.

The honest truth of the matter is that it is not enough to have the right things in your life. The real root of greatness is the *right thing* at the *right time*. Seasons of being held up or stuck are not meant to drain and frustrate you, but rather to develop you in every area of your life. These fragile moments should be used to showcase the glory of God in your life.

Praise God and pray more in these times. Never take God keeping you in the same place as permission to become lazy. Take the season as an opportunity to put him and his strength on display as you build your own strength for the next season. The motto of our lives in the middle of transition ought to be this: If it is not the right time, I will refuse the right thing.

The Bible is full of accounts of people who were hindered in their progress because of their lack of trust in God. However, it also contains many accounts of those who experienced the fullness of their purpose and destiny because of their trust in God and his ultimate plan for their lives.

The book of Hebrews outlines these examples in its famous "hall of faith" chapter (Hebrews 11). This chapter shows us what notable figures like Noah, Abraham, and Moses shared in common with lesser-known figures such as Enoch, Barak, or Jephthah: Their faith (what I call "tremendous trust") caused them to do the very thing for which they were created at the exact time they were created to do it.

Those mentioned in this awe-inspiring chapter persevered in his-torically troubled and tragic times long enough to transition into the greatness we glorify when retelling their supernatural stories. We celebrate their example of faith but often fail to celebrate the audacious amount of trust it took for them to see God's plan through to the end.

The same is true of you. I wonder what stories will be told of your fierce faith and exceedingly great trust in God's plan. They may not be so much about how you were stuck as much as how God used your stuck situations to write your stories from the very elements it is taking to simply hold on in your current condition. I wonder what others will read about you of which you are not yet aware. I wonder what is in God's mind that has not even entered into your own heart yet. I know you are hanging in there now, but keep hanging in there. God is more than interested and invested in the outcome, and he is banking on the fact that you will get off that cross and move toward that resurrection moment. He is willing to reveal to you and use on your behalf every resource necessary to make it happen.

Do more than get your head up or your hopes up. Get your trust up. I promise you that God will exceed your expectations. The transition has transformed you. Now allow the trust it has produced to move you.

Now that transformation and trust formation are over, the real question emerges: Are you ready to move?

Chapter 6

A Guy Named Joseph: Transition Has Help

My parents warned me to stay put. They emphatically said, "It is only going to get worse." Still, my know-it-all, twenty-one-year-old self refused to listen. I started my journey from the small church in West Virginia where I began ministry as a youth pastor back to my home, forty-five minutes away, in Maryland.

As I began, the roads were merely dusted with snow and I snickered at my parents' advice and countless phone calls to check in. Around the twentieth phone call (I am exaggerating) I started down a steep hill. I had not noticed that the snowfall had increased significantly and the below freezing temps had made the roads extra icy. Even at ten miles an hour, my car lost traction and tapped the guardrail. I did not dare hit the gas and had no chance at backing up. My parents had been proven right. I was STUCK! I nervously dialed my parents with my pride crushed, fearing something worse might happen as a result of my poor decision making.

My mother answered my call, and I mumbled what had happened to me. To my surprise, I did not hear anger from them. Instead, my mom told me to stay calm. The most surprising thing was that by the end of my phone call, which lasted about three minutes, my mother reported that my father had already called my grandparents and uncle who lived approximately five miles away from where I was stuck. My mother ended the call by saying, "Stay there. Help is on the way!" Within minutes, my uncle and grandfather arrived with the tools and means to get me out of a terrible stuck situation to a place of safety.

I will never forget that moment in my life. I certainly will not forget the fear associated with my bad decision. I kept replaying it in my head, thankful I was not dead, yet baffled I had ever done such a stupid thing.

Lesson Learned

I will never forget the life lesson I learned that night, and I will certainly never lose the impact of the spiritual lesson I learned. That night took me to the school of God's grace and mercy towards me. The more I reflected on what could have happened, the more I was overwhelmed with thanksgiving to God for all the harm from which he had spared me.

I realize that some people do not make it through the kind of moment I experienced that night. My existence beyond the trouble is the reason I do not hesitate to give God thanks. It is the reason I praise God passionately and worship him unashamedly.

Take a second here to reflect on not what you have been through (as we have already done that in this book), but to reflect on the goodness, faithfulness, mercy, and grace of God. He is truly a good God.

Help Me

As I write this chapter I can also see the next step in the process of transition. My near tragic accident had given me a firsthand glimpse of a lesson on transition that I am only beginning to understand right now.

That night showed me that my bad decision put me in a bad situation. That one choice put me in a spot I had never intended or wanted to be in. Unknowingly, the bad spot put me in a great position to respond correctly. I called my parents. My phone call not only got them involved, but also released much needed help from a source that was closer than I thought.

Take this one step further. There are times when we make choices, and those choices affect us by positioning us in places we may or may not want to be. However, as we have discussed, our God is working all things together for our good and for his purpose.

The thing we often miss is the opportunity to respond correctly in our moment of distress. We choose to stay stuck! However, this is our transition's next prerequisite.

Transition will always require a response. It ought to prompt us to call our Heavenly Father. I think we would be shocked to see God's response behind the scenes when we cry out to him from the midst of our trouble and confusion. After all, one of the Bible's great promises to us is that God is our present help in times of trouble (Psalm 46:1). I think we would find that God is as anxious to help us move on from our trouble as we are to get out of it. I think we would be amazed at the resources God has waiting to become our rescue. The key is to invite him in and ask him for help.

"Transition will always require a response."

Into Your Hands

As Jesus ended his earthly life, he uttered words that speak loudly to this point. In the closing moments of his life, he said, "Father, into Your hands I commit My spirit." (Luke 23:46) Did you catch that? The words of Jesus were more than a declaration of death, they were permission for God to begin the next thing. To get there, Jesus knew he would need his Father's heavenly help.

". . . God is as anxious to help us move on from our trouble as we are to get out of it."

This is the right response: "Into your hands, Lord, I give you my life!" What looked like an end in the natural world was the beginning of a movement in the spiritual world for Jesus. The resources of heaven were unleashed, natural and supernatural, and headed in Jesus's direction.

Right now, before going any further, I feel so burdened to stop and simply tell you to call on God. Ask God for help. It is time for you to understand that it is not selfish to ask God for anything. Asking God for his involvement is a great compliment to our Heavenly Father. Our requests to God are not selfish, for two reasons. First, they declare that we do not have the means to do for ourselves what we are asking. In other words, our requests say we cannot do it! Second, our requests acknowledge the fact that what we need, God does have the means to provide. We are saying we cannot do it, but he can!

I am here to tell you that God can! Elevate your faith, open up your mouth, and invite God in. God is a good God, a faithful Father who promised not to leave us or forsake us (Deuteronomy 31:8). This promise only further establishes the fact that God is willing and able to help.

Poured Out Blessings

My entire life has been filled with faith-filled vocabulary. From the earliest time I can remember, I constantly and consistently heard my parents, grandparents, aunts, and uncles speak words of faith to each other. This kind of talk was a big part of my everyday life. I can distinctly remember every morning, before we left for school, we started with prayer and positive confession of who God is and what we expected him to do.

However, of the entire Christian vernacular used in our household, one statement seemed to be used more than others. In fact, I heard it so much, I could recite it in my sleep. In my mind, I can still hear my father say with fervor and power, "God, we thank you for all the blessings you have poured out upon our family."

Poured out blessings? What did that even mean? As a kid, I thought this was tied to the proverbial cup I was to give the Lord so he could fill it up. Only as I have progressed in age have I begun to understand the context of what my family had declared in regard to those poured out blessings.

Biblically, I understand where my family got the statement. They had grabbed it from the Old Testament book of Malachi, embedded in one of the most popular verses of Scripture, Malachi 3:10 (NKJV), which tells us that God would, *"open for you the windows of heaven and pour out for you such blessing, that there will not be room enough to receive it."*

Up until this recent revelation, the only takeaway I had from this scripture is that God had big blessings that exceeded my own personal capacity to receive them. While there is no real problem with that exegetical analysis, at its best, the takeaway is true but incomplete. On a deeper level, there is more to be seen and understood. I had only looked at the size of the blessing, and in doing so, failed to realize that behind the size was the something even more glorious—the substance of the blessing.

God's blessings are indeed poured out blessings. There is beauty in the fact that God gives his blessings fluidity. Poured out blessings are not prepackaged from some supernatural assembly line in heaven. They are personally manufactured by God to fit each person's personal needs. So when the time is right and the condition of man's obedience is completed, God simply and methodically . . . pours it out.

The revelation of "poured out blessings" is life-changing. It is life-changing because it yields this emphatic truth: *because it is poured, the blessing takes the mold of whatever it has been poured upon.* This means that God's poured blessings are small enough to be poured onto the material blessing of a check, and yet sizable enough to be poured onto a home, car, or bank account.

Poured out blessings can even take the mold of a person! Sometimes, when God pours you out a blessing it can come in the form of a person instead of a thing. No matter what the blessing falls on—whether big or small—it is always substantial. Not because of how it comes, but because of who poured it and where it comes from.

The only requirement to receive these "poured out blessings" from God is discernment. If discernment is not present during the pouring, we will look at the packaging God has put the blessing in and walk past the blessing the packaging contains. This is where prayer comes in. Prayer is the easiest way to gain the discernment necessary to understand whether what has walked into your life in this transitional season is a blessing or a lesson. It is this discernment that allows us to, as Malachi 3:10 exhorts, make room for the blessing God has poured out for us. Any blessing for which you do not have discernment, you certainly will not have room enough to receive.

Your transition depends on your understanding of this principle. As you journey, God will sovereignly bless you between where you have been and where you are going. These blessings are indicators—mile markers and flag posts—telling you to keep moving in the current direction you are heading. The blessing, because of its fluidity, may fall on the most unlikely of people and things. With discernment, God will let you know that he has your back, he is your help, and he will sustain you in your transition season.

Back to the Passage

Here is where our key passage in John 19 becomes precious to this part of the transition process. An invitation for God's help is often met with a release of resources. The disciple John writes: "After this, Joseph of Arimathea, being a disciple of Jesus, but secretly, for fear of the Jews, asked Pilate that he might take away the body of Jesus; and Pilate gave him permission" (John 19:38).

The disciple Jesus loved, John, gives us the detail that upon the *after this* of Jesus, a resource for a movement was released. A resource in the form of a new character came on the scene: Joseph of Arimathea. Other than coming up in a game of Bible Trivia you played, you may never have even heard of him. There is no doubt that this Joseph takes a backseat to the Joseph with the coat of many colors, written of in the book of Genesis. He is by no means as popular as Joseph the carpenter, the nonbiological father of Jesus. However, this is the Joseph God uses to take Jesus from the place of his greatest pain to the place of his glorious resurrection. This lesser-known Joseph is certainly not any less important. This man would prove to be the vehicle to victory for Jesus.

Vehicle to Victory

This detail alone should cause our hope to skyrocket. If God sent Jesus a Joseph to carry him from his cross, then he has a vehicle to victory for you, too. God has the help you need, and make no mistake; his help is on the way. He has the resources to not only remove your pain, but to chauffeur you to your ultimate glory.

"God has the help you need, and make no mistake; his help is on the way. He has the resources to not only remove your pain, but to chauffeur you to your ultimate glory."

Before we take a praise break, I will give you one more thing to shout about. John writes that Joseph was a "disciple of Jesus, but secretly" (John 19:38). The *after this* of Jesus was so powerful that it literally drew a secret believer out of hiding. Jesus's death inspired Joseph, a member of the Sanhedrin (the religious group that crucified Christ), to come out of the shadows.

Joseph was a secret disciple until the right moment. In other words, God's resource was a hidden one . . . until just the perfect time. At the perfect time, Joseph came running out from his private discipleship into a public relationship.

Joseph was more than burdened by what he saw—he was inspired. God had let Jesus's tragedy motivate Joseph to action. In the middle of transition, you will find yourself on both sides of this spectrum. This is the beauty of the sovereignty of God. In some moments, you will be on the receiving end of help (Jesus). In other moments, you will be the person God uses, inspires, and motivates to be the help someone else so desperately needs (Joseph).

Hidden Help

No one counted on a prestigious member of the Sanhedrin becoming God's source of help. As mentioned, Joseph was a disciple in secret, an ally in anonymity. Joseph was God's secret weapon who came from a place no one thought, to help in a way no one else could.

The same is true for you! God has hidden and secret resources for you. They are waiting for the final breaths of the past to be breathed. They are inspired to come out of hiding by your declaration of surrender and obedience. They are watching to see if you will place the rest of your life and your transition into the very hands of God. They are your help! They are your vehicles to victory. While your help may not be named Joseph, I promise it will have a name, and it will bring your answer. It will propel you forward. Most importantly, it will enable you to get through your transition so you can live in your resurrection.

If help is on the way, take time to pray for discernment to understand and recognize the help you have been sent. Use your prayer time to let God speak clearly so that you only connect with what God has sent.

Make no bones about it; when God sends it, hell and its devious plans cannot stop it. If hell could not stop it, a man named Pilate certainly could not either. I hope you are packed because it is moving day for your destiny.

Chapter 7

Permission to Move: The Permission Slip of Transition

You were not called to live on it . . . plain and simple. You were never meant to live *there*! Where is there? "There" is your cross. "There" is your crucifixion season. "There" is the situation, circumstance, curse, or issue you have been attached to in the previous season of your life. When it comes to transition, nothing will hold you back more than setting up a permanent address in a place God intended to be a temporary home.

The cross of Calvary was not meant to be a forever place for Jesus. It was designed to be a temporary location to accomplish a God sized purpose. Contrary to what some would say, the cross was not *the entire plan*, but it was a crucial part of it. God's intention was not that the cross would be the final resting place of Jesus's life and purpose. It was only a part of the process. Get this truth in your heart, mind, and spirit. God never intended your cross to be the place where you would live, or the place upon which you would build the rest of your life. It was to be the launching pad by which you would soar into your destiny.

Carry It

The biblical answer for the question of your personal cross is simple. You were not designed to live on the cross; you were called to carry it. The Bible is clear on this in Matthew 16:24, when Jesus said, "If anyone desires to come after Me, let him deny himself, and take up his cross, and follow Me." Mark, another of Christ's disciples heard it verbatim in

Mark 8:34 and repeats it in his gospel by saying, "Whoever desires to come after Me, let him deny himself, and take up *his cross*, and follow Me" (emphasis added).

The disciples are making a clear and distinct point here. They are saying emphatically that the cross was never meant to be lived upon because we have been called to carry it. On the surface, carrying our cross seems unnecessary and is undoubtedly a heavy burden to bear. However, the more I stare intently at this text, the more I see a grand opportunity for believers.

We do not carry this cross as a means of remaining attached to our pain or past, but as an opportunity to display victory over the things that once had us bound. Carrying our cross affords us the opportunity to showcase that we now rule over the very things that ruled over us. It is a display that we now have the very issue that used to have us! It is the spoils of our battle and the trophy of our tragedies.

"We do not carry this cross as a means of remaining attached to our pain or past, but as an opportunity to display victory over the things that once had us bound."

Off the Cross, On to Victory

There is always a moment in transition when you come down off your cross. It is a moment of release and complete freedom from your *after this*. It is a moment that speaks to you, saying you have outlasted the pain and survived the storm. This is a moment that becomes the permission slip for you to walk in total victory. So before you build a mailbox and stamp an address on the letters to your future from the place of your former pain and negative circumstances, understand God has given you permission to move. The permission slip has been signed so you can now move into what is next.

Moving Day

> After this, Joseph of Arimathea, being a disciple of Jesus, but secretly, for fear of the Jews, asked Pilate that he might take away the body of Jesus; and Pilate gave *him* permission. (John 19:38)

As the purpose of the cross was accomplished, an understanding of who Christ had been was communicated. He was who he said he was. He was, indeed, the Son of God sent to save a broken and lost humanity. Even as Christ's body hung lifeless on the cross, God sent the resources for progress. Joseph had been moved upon by God and responded to the call. Everything in that moment was saying the same thing. Jesus was ready! It was moving day.

As we continue to take the next steps in transition and methodically move through the biblical text in the Gospel of John, we suddenly come to a keen awareness of something more. Not only is Jesus ready to move, he is also perfectly positioned to graduate into his next moment of movement within his purpose.

A phrase toward the end of John 19:38 caught my attention; where it says Pilate "gave him permission." It was the final obstacle to finally moving forward. Though I could write quite a bit about this, I will summarize it with this: If Joseph had not come when he did to move the body of Jesus, Jesus would have run the risk of someone else mishandling or moving him—quite possibly to the wrong place. Had that happened, Jesus would have been close, yet so very far away from fulfilling Old Testament prophecy, and would have ultimately been delayed in his purpose.

Relationships and Permission Slips

This is why relationships are crucial. They all take us somewhere and affect us in some way. The sooner you can come to grips with the intentions, agendas, and motivations of whatever or whoever has walked into your life, the quicker you will be able to be on your way to where you are called to be.

The goal of any relationship is to identify it, name it, and discern where it will ultimately take us if we choose to follow it and have fellowship with it. I wonder how differently our lives would look (and play out) if this was our approach to every new relationship. I am curious to know the trouble and heartache we would avoid if we were not so quick to make decisions and used our discernment before walking down the road with those who claim to have come with help.

The truth is you must trace the path before you walk it. The danger of a relationship is often not seen on the surface. Therefore, it is wise to pray,

take your time, and increase your knowledge and understanding of someone before committing yourself to them. It can take months and even years
to recover from the tragic fallout of committing to a wrong relationship.

**"The goal of any relationship is to identify it, name it, and
discern where it will ultimately take us if we choose to
follow it and have fellowship with it."**

Can I See Your ID?

The bottom line is that you must discern who comes to help you move.
There are three crucial relationships that will make themselves avail-
able to you at the moment you are ready to move in your transition. In
light of our text in John, I will call them "Pilates," "Pharisees and Sadducees," and "Josephs."

Pilates

Everyone knows the Pilate of your life. Pilate was there for your sen-
tencing, there while you stood at the mercy of your circumstances, and
surprisingly, even possibly had a part in preventing some of your pain.
However, Pilate, while he had the power to do something significant, did
not do enough to make a difference.

Pilates are the people in your life who did not like what was happening to you, but let it happen anyway. Who are the Pilates in your life who
could have helped but did not? They knew to do one thing concerning
you—the right thing—but ended up doing another. One of the most concerning attributes of the Pilates of your life is that they are there, just not
when you need them to act on your behalf.

Perhaps Pilate's most defining characteristic is pinpointed when the
Bible says he "washed his hands" concerning Jesus (Matthew 27:24).
The most hurtful thing that can happen to you in the middle of a crisis
is a person you thought cared about you washes his or her hands of you
and what is happening to you. It is a heartbreaking thing to go through
painful times alone, and Pilates will let you do so. Do not worry though.
Pilates are not your answer, though they could have been.

Pharisees and Sadducees

In Bible times, these guys were notorious for all the wrong reasons. These two groups made up the one governmental and religious leadership group called the Sanhedrin. The Sanhedrin prided themselves on self-righteousness and keeping the law.

This made Jesus enemy number one. He constantly and consistently brought to light their hidden issues and agendas, ultimately causing them to conspire against him, culminating in his crucifixion. The Pharisees wanted one thing: Punishment. They were present throughout Christ's torturous beating and crucifixion. To them, Jesus had it coming. To them, Jesus was a heretic bent on destroying Judaism. He had to be stopped at all cost. His mission could by no means succeed. They were the resistance against Jesus.

Does any of this sound familiar to you? All of us have felt the resistance and opposition of these people to the mission to which God called us and sent us to do. Pharisees and Sadducees are the people in your life who commit themselves to buying front row seats to your failures. They are angry at your success and find fault in all the good you do and accomplish. However, the worst thing about relationships with Pharisees and Sadducees just might be that even if you endure their punishment and achieve something great, they will work tirelessly to make sure no one knows it ever happened.

Knowing that there are true enemies to your transitions is another heartbreaking element of the entire process. It is always hard to believe that others have made it their purpose to stop yours. But thanks be to God that he always causes you to triumph (2 Corinthians 2:14). It is wonderful to know that if God is for you, no one can stand against you (Romans 8:31), and that no weapon formed against you will succeed (Isaiah 54:17). It is a blessing to know that the one who is in you is greater than the devil or any enemy of yours in the world (1 John 4:4).

Do not worry about the Pharisees and Sadducees. They do not have the final say on you, your life, or what God has called you to be or do. No matter what their intentions may be, they will not override God's plan and purpose for you.

Josephs

Ah, finally, the relationships that are most necessary to your transition; the ones that matter most for you to live out your purpose. Josephs are sent to you by God to get you out. They are the helping for which you have been praying and asking God. They are an answer to your *after this.*

Everyone needs at least one Joseph—*everyone!* They come from unusual places with a common purpose; to help you move. Pilate would have left Jesus. The Pharisees and Sadducees would have hid or mishandled Jesus. However, Joseph was faithful to do what God sent him to do, and moved Jesus's body, positioning him for his next great thing.

The Josephs in your life come to do the same thing. They are only interested in seeing you go forward. They are not committed to talking about your past or keeping you pinned to former mistakes. They are there for you to see you move.

Josephs motivate you to keep going. They rarely let you settle for anything less than God's best. As you are reading, you are undoubtedly thinking of a Joseph in your life. Once you have identified the Pilates, Pharisees and Sadducees, you will see that the Josephs, like cream, rise to the top.

Thank God for the Josephs in your life. They are essential to your successful navigation of the transitions of life. They are crucial to getting you from here to there. They are the truest definition of being "God sent." They are invested in you and your purpose.

I encourage you to take some time to thank your Josephs. Identify the Josephs that came to your rescue and kept you moving toward your destiny. Write them a card or take them out dinner and thank them. Whatever you do, appreciate them for being exactly what you needed to keep moving in the direction of your purpose.

Without the tenacity of a Joseph, Jesus might have been left where he was or been moved to the wrong place. Without our Josephs, we may well have found ourselves far away from fulfilling our purpose. Sadly, many of us have been mishandled or "left for dead" by bad relationships. If this happened to you, I have good news for you: God still knows who to use and how to move you. You are on your way! Do not stop now. Right now is just the start of your new beginning.

Chapter 8

Buried? Transition and Burial

And Nicodemus, who at first came to Jesus by night, also
came, bringing a mixture of myrrh and aloes, about a
hundred pounds. 40 Then they took the body of Jesus,
and bound it in strips of linen with the spices, *as the custom of the Jews is to bury.*

(John 19:39-40, emphasis added)

The road to a successful transition is never easy. It holds surprises
around every corner. Just as soon as you think you can breathe and settle, you are hit with the unexpected.

Once again, transition requires trust . . . a significant amount of trust.
Thus far, our journey has been full of trust filled moments and trust filled
places where the goodness of God in our yesterday became the faith we
needed to continue to follow him into our tomorrow.

Sometimes, as we get free from our last season we find that we have
not yet fully embraced the process of the next season. We are so ecstatic
to be *moving on* that we are unsure what it is going to take to *move in*
to the next thing. As brutal as our crucifixion seasons are, and as glorious as the moment of understanding why we went through them is, we
often find ourselves seemingly unprepared with a to-do list to prepare
for what is next.

The bottom line is no one, including God, said that what is next in the
process of your transition was going to be fun or easy. He just promised

that it was necessary for the next season and level of glory to be seen in your life (2 Corinthians 4:17).

Burial?

Our passage of scripture does more than show us Jesus's death; it lets us in on his continued movement beyond the cross. Joseph has moved him and his crucifixion has officially come to a conclusion. Perfect! Get out the cake and candles, and put on your party hats: It is time to celebrate. In fact, just close this book and call it a day. There is no need for you to read on; just grab a Starbucks and take a bubble bath. (Okay, too far.)

As good as all of the previously mentioned things sound, we cannot quit here. We cannot quit here because this is not the end. Transition is twofold. More than being just about finishing the worst moments of your life, transition is about starting the new season of preparation for the best.

"Transition is twofold. More than being just about finishing the worst moments of your life, transition is about starting the new season of preparation for the best."

When help arrived in the form of Joseph of Arimathea, Jesus's transition had just begun. Joseph was moving Jesus to his ultimate place of preparation. Joseph was not escorting Jesus to the Jerusalem Hilton or an all-expense paid getaway on some tropical island. He was transporting Jesus to a place of *burial.*

Is It Necessary to Be Buried?

Just when it seemed like the roller coaster was on its way back up and things were going to get infinitely better, another corkscrew was unleashed, taking our key story and passage to an all-time low.

Burial? Why? What are burial seasons, and what good can possibly come from someone being buried? The burial season is the place of preparation and the space in time between where you were last and where you are supposed to be next. In the passion week of Christ it was nearly three days.

Burial seasons are often the least spoken of yet the longest seasons in destiny. Hidden in them is healing from yesterday and preparation for tomorrow. Undoubtedly, burial is necessary. There is no way of getting around this if you want to walk in your purpose. It is a place you must come to grips with as you navigate the world of transition. Without it, destiny will always be a distant theory, but never a true reality.

"Burial seasons are often the least spoken of yet the longest seasons in destiny. Hidden in them is healing from yesterday and preparation for tomorrow."

Have you ever escaped a situation or circumstance and thought, *Whew that was close, but I made it out alive,* only to get slammed with a new seemingly negative reality that, according to God, is working for your good? This is where we are in our journey called transition. Quite possibly, this is where you are in yours.

This Looks Bad

As I read this part of the passage I could not help but think, *How can something so God (burial), look like something so bad?* The tension of the scriptures I was reading was by no means breathtaking and by all means heartbreaking. All the prophecies from the mouth of our savior to his disciples about building his kingdom and rebuilding the temple were crumbling before my eyes and becoming increasingly hard to believe. After all, he was dead and now they were preparing him to go into a tomb. Jesus was not just down, he was soon to be out.

It was out of this moment of study and prayer that I got extremely bold with God. I said aloud: "God, this is bad! Your Son is down and now it seems like you are about to let him be taken out. If this is a picture of us, and we are called to imitate Christ, then I have to ask, why must I get buried?" I had no idea what answer waited within my question; all I know is I was glad I asked.

Get in That Tomb

I am learning that God's answers are often found in my questions. Most of the time we do not hear an answer because somewhere along the way we thought (or were taught) we cannot question God. Do not believe that lie. Ask away. Revelation is often hidden inside asking the right questions.

So why must we be buried? It is not enough for me to say, "Because Jesus was," although that was the answer that earned me the most candy in Sunday school. It was not sufficient for me to say, "Because the Bible says so." Before I answer the question, you must view the process of the burial season as crucial to your transition and the entire transition process.

The truth of the matter is, if you have not embraced your burial season you have not really embraced your transition. There are three reasons for burial that will help answer this difficult question, ease your worries, and reveal God's intention and truth concerning burial and the burial seasons of life.

So, why . . . why must we be buried?

It Proves Your Dead

In ministry, I have yet to attend any funeral or graveside service where the body in the casket was still living. The funeral and graveside settles and puts to rest any thought that the person in the casket is still alive.

For some, what I just wrote is assumed and obvious, but for those of us navigating transition, this is a life-giving spiritual revelation. The death of flesh I am speaking about is by no means physical, but completely spiritual. The benefit of surrendering to the burial season is a declaration of death; death to the flesh and the rule of our carnal nature over our decisions and desires.

We battle our flesh continually. Our flesh asks us to do things that are contrary to the very character of God. Our flesh would have us do what we do not wish to do and not do the things we want to do (Romans 7:15-25). Falling prey to the whims of the flesh can obstruct us or distract us from all God wants us to accomplish concerning his will. We can be misled and form bad relationships and friendships, get pulled into wrong career choices, view God's path with blurred vision, or hear only muffled sounds when listening for his voice.

We must be buried. Burial renders the flesh powerless and turns loose the spirit man to take complete control of your life and all its decisions. The Spirit led life is the one God intended for the believer so that he or she could be truly guided into God's best in every season. Wherever you are going in God, you cannot afford to be controlled by your flesh. Only burial can truly lay it to rest.

"We must be buried. Burial renders the flesh powerless and turns loose the spirit man to take complete control of your life and all its decisions."

It Brings Finality to Your Crucifixion

Finally, it is over, and burial is the way you can put a period at the end of the sentence on your crucifixion season. I am unsure of the reason why, but there are people in your life who will not mind reminding you of where you have been, and frankly, do not mind keeping you pinned to your pain.

Those "haters" (in modern vernacular) are often jealous of your movement. Your success indicts their very place of residence, to their mind. In other words, when you move, it will expose their lack of movement. Whenever you go higher or move forward, some people will work to keep you in your former season. It may come in the form of a phone call, text, or email, but the objective of the conversation is the same: They want to keep your mind in your former season.

The mind is a powerful thing. In Proverbs 23:7 the Bible declares of men (people), "as he thinks in his heart, so *is* he." Burial closes the season of opportunity for the voices of your haters and enemies to be heard. The closing of the coffin and barring of the tomb will silence your foes and declare that you have moved on, and they need to as well!

It Is Impossible to Have a Resurrection without It

Finally, possibly the most important reason for a burial season is that, without it, there can be no resurrection. Resurrection is not a possibility for the living. Only the dead can be resurrected. To explain it another way: You cannot have an incredible resurrection until you have first had a proper burial.

The death I am focusing on here is spiritual death to your flesh. The burial season we are focusing on is a means of transition and transportation to your destiny. The burial season becomes imperative once you realize it will assist in your resurrection moment. Burial is a must.

"You cannot have an incredible resurrection until you have first had a proper burial."

If God is taking you into a season of burial, get excited. The season of burial may feel extreme—even unnecessary—but make no mistake; it is the gateway to God's glory being seen in and on your life. If you can persevere through the burial seasons of life, your transition to resurrection is 100 percent imminent.

I challenge you to submit to this part of the process. Do not let the fear of the burial season keep you from taking the next step. Submit to God. Pray this prayer right now:

Father, you have brought me to this place. You have proven over and over in this process that you care for me. You have protected me, delivered me, and even helped me reach this place. Now I ask you to help ease my fears and doubts as I submit to this part of the process—my burial season. I know I can trust you and that you are preparing me for the very thing for which I was created. Hide me so that I may never hide you. In Jesus's name, amen.

Are you ready to be buried? The hour of your crucifixion is complete and the dawn of your new day is closer than you think. Let what God sent to help you do, do what he assigned it to do. It has been sent on assignment, and is prepared to prepare you for what God has already prepared for you. It is time for burial.

Chapter 9

Making Preparation: Steps to a Successful Burial

And Nicodemus, who at first came to Jesus by night, also came, bringing a mixture of myrrh and aloes, about a hundred pounds. Then they took the body of Jesus, and bound it in strips of linen with the spices, as the custom of the Jews is to bury.

(John 19:39-40)

To say I grew up in church is an understatement. I could say the church was my second home. I lived in church. I do believe that if any thieves wanted to break into the Carter residence, they could easily have done so by breaking in on Sunday mornings, Sunday evenings, and Wednesday evenings. Church was life.

To be honest, growing up, I loved church. I loved Sunday school, the services, and seeing my friends. Perhaps more than the sermon, I loved the worship. Now worship in the 90s looked nothing like today's worship. We had no blazing lights or professional worship ministers. We did not even have words on screens! We simply had a song leader (my grandfather), a red covered hymnal, and a group of hungry people ready to worship. It blessed me.

We sang many of what we would call "traditional" hymns, but I can remember distinctly adding what some of the older folks called praise choruses to the Sunday morning praise and worship. It was one of these "praise choruses" that became one of my favorite songs to sing to this day. The chorus went like this:

> Lord prepare me, to be a sanctuary, pure and holy, tried and true, and with thanksgiving, I'll be a living, sanctuary, for you.

> ("Sanctuary," by Randy Lynn Scruggs and John W. Thompson Copyright © 1983 by Whole Armor Publishing Company and Full Armor Publishing Company. Administered by Peermusic III, Ltd. Used By Permission. All Rights Reserved)

Lord Prepare Me

Singing this song was a reality check for me. I had only ever asked the Lord to use me. This song was begging me to make another level of commitment.

"Lord, prepare me." What a tremendous suggestion and thought. I remember being captivated by these three words in this simple chorus. In spite of its simplicity, however, I realized it held a significant truth to which I needed to surrender.

As I am now in full-time ministry, I am aware of the weight of the words, "Lord prepare me," more than ever before. Preparation is God's intended process for us between seasons. We ought never wait between seasons; we ought to prepare for the next season.

A significant question arises: How do I prepare for what is next when I do not know what is next? The answer is simple: *Lord*, prepare me. By all means, we should be active in the preparation process God gives us in the middle of our burial season. We should pray and read our Bibles, and we should attend church. We must do our part. However, for what we don't know we must simply say: *Lord*, prepare me. And one key piece of proper preparation is making sure we place ourselves in the proper position.

Lord Position Me

God does his greatest preparations by utilizing whatever is in proper position. Whether a burning bush on the backside of the desert for

Moses, a wilderness for the children of Israel, a shepherd's field for a boy named David, or an upper room for twelve disciples, the Bible is explicit in helping us understand that preparation needs the right person in the right place in the right position. The ultimate reason proper position is key to necessary preparation is that burial is not an ending but a beautiful beginning. Jewish culture sees death this way—an open door to eternity, not a dead end.

Jesus was no different. With the cross behind him and the tomb of burial before him all that was left was proper burial preparation to enter into a new beginning. When the day came to an end, Jesus's body was in the hands of those ready to prepare him for burial and place him in a sepulcher.

John writes of the exact preparations in his accounts of Joseph of Arimathea and Nicodemus. In John 3:1-21 he describes the encounter between Jesus and Nicodemus, which gives us what is arguably the most popular verse in all of scripture, John 3:16. This Pharisee once again comes at the evening hour, but this time to assist Joseph in the burial preparations for Jesus's body.

According to our key passage, Nicodemus's gift to the burial preparation was a mixture of myrrh and aloes. Before I break down the purpose of this specific part of the preparation, I want you to understand that those God has sent into your life for this season all bring something specific, yet valuable to the process. The right people in your life will heal the hurts of your tragedies and traumas while the wrong people will have no problem keeping your festering wounds from the past open and painful. Be sure to recognize the value in each of these people who bring gifts that heal, and welcome them and their unique gifts into your life.

Products of a Proper Preparation

There were three parts to burial preparation in that culture in that time. All three are found in our key passage, which provides God's blueprint for your preparation for your new beginning. In every burial season you will need these unique gifts. God sends these to you in ways you cannot do yourself. They are perfect additions for your new beginning.

Apply Aloes and Myrrh

When the body of Jesus was removed from the cross, the wounds from the trauma of the torturous beating he had endured and brutal death on the cross he had suffered still remained. The trauma of Calvary was over, but the reminders of the trauma were written in stripes on his back and nail prints on his hands and feet.

The bruised and battered body of Jesus had been ripped open by the weapons of his enemies. Two Pharisees held in their hands the elements and implements needed to bring healing to a body that had been battered. Both aloe and myrrh are known to bring healing.

Do you see the beauty in this fact? Before any other preparation steps were taken, the first step involved healing the wounds inflicted as part of the cruel suffering of the cross. But why? Why would you apply healing agents to a body that has ceased to carry life? What good is it to dress a wound that is no longer bleeding? Is there a purpose in tending to pain that is no longer felt by the victim? On the surface, the answer is easy: No. However, is it possible that these *believers* knew something that most did not? Did they understand that his death was momentary and that these very wounds and scars would be used as evidence to prove his death and resurrection beyond the tomb? (John 20:20; Luke 24:36-43) The Bible is not explicit on the matter, but something in me believes they knew that Jesus was not finished and that the healing virtue of the aloes and myrrh needed to be applied to the body of Jesus for what was about to happen next.

God is not in the business of sending you into the next season unwell and not whole. This does not mean there are no scars; it simply means nothing is festering or open. God's healing in our lives often brings closure to the pain of our past. In fact, when God brings emotional healing, he does not remove the experience, memory, or even the scars, but validates the healing by removing the pain. This is the purpose of the aloe and myrrh. They mend the open wounds suffered at the hands of those who afflicted us, leaving us whole and unable to become bitter, angry, or frustrated in the fresh and new season of our purpose. You need more than to be moved in burial seasons, you need to be made whole .

Though myrrh was used as a healing agent, it was also used as incense for embalming, replacing even the stench of death with the fragrance of life. Once again, a valuable and beautiful revelation rises from the pages of Scripture to us. God is gracious enough to not just heal the wounds of our crucifixion, but also to remove the stench of the effects of our crucifixion season. When God does this, it baffles the enemies of our lives and makes bystanders curious. The people who watched our lives and seen our trauma do not detect from our scent that we had ever experienced it. Only God can erase the scent of tragedy and replace it with the scent of abundant life.

As incredible as both myrrh and aloes are, however, the purpose for combining the two presents the greatest revelation. More than healing and removing the stench of death, the two come together for a greater purpose . . . preventing decay.

This is what the enemy wants. Beyond the cross, our adversary wants us to move into a season of decay. Our enemy wants our gifts to decay, our relationships to decay, and certainly our dreams to decay. However, when the aloes and myrrh are applied, they become the enemy of decay and the agent of preservation.

The healing of your wounds and the new scent of abundant life are the preservation agents of your resurrection. These will keep your dreams alive and your gifts functional. Let the Josephs and Nicodemuses apply the herbs of aloe and myrrh, and watch the healing begin and your purpose unfold.

Dress in Linen

Linens? Those are the good clothes, right? I mean, everyone wants to be buried in their "Sunday best," but is that not a waste of good material? The questions you just read are the questions I asked when I read this part of the key scripture. I just found it hard to rationalize putting something that nice on something that dead.

The passage says that Joseph and Nicodemus wrapped the clean and preserved body of Jesus in strips of linen. They were dressing Jesus for burial. The tattered and bloody garments of his crucifixion—the clothing of yesterday—had been stripped from him and replaced with fresh linens of his tomorrow.

How profound! Joseph and Nicodemus were not dressing him based on where he had been; they were dressing him based on where he was going. With the change of garments they were establishing a new and fresh identity based on Jesus's destiny, not his history.

This is step two of your preparation. After the healing of the aloes comes the linens of fresh identity. The freshness of the linens is more than a picture of the new identity, it is a picture of a fresh start. It is God's way of saying you were "that," but with the new clothes he provides, you can become "this." I wonder what new identity God is giving you with the help of men and women of God he has placed in your life.

Every Sunday, your pastor or minister is doing more than preaching you a cute sermon; he or she is dressing you for destiny. The words of the sermon are clothing you with God-breathed truths about you and your future. The best place to be on a Sunday morning is in the fitting room called God's house where, each week, he is tailoring you for your destiny.

This is the truest definition of being dressed for success; letting God place his identity for you, on you. This is the place of letting go of perspectives and opinions that have clung to you through all you have been through and being elegantly dressed by the Word of God.

A wardrobe change is necessary for your next season. The sooner you can get dressed, the closer you will be to walking out the newly assigned purpose for your life.

Bind It Up

This is step three, and the last part of burial preparation. While it is last on this list, it is certainly not the least. After applying the aloes and myrrh, and adding the linens, we find Joseph and Nicodemus doing something seemingly odd, given the situation. The Bible says that the two Pharisees turned followers bound the body of Jesus. To me, this is odd for the simple fact that Jesus is indeed dead. His body is lifeless and unable to move.

As odd as this may be, the revelation is stunning. Binding the body was another way of placing the finishing touches on the positioning of the body. Binding the body was the only sure way to set Jesus up for a divine resurrection at a divinely perfect time. By the time Joseph and Nicodemus were finished, this body could not move, even if it wanted to. The only way to get out of the tomb would be through divine intervention.

Transition longs for divine intervention, a moment at which all preparation shifts into a season of hibernation. As humans with carnal minds and deviant flesh, we often seek to do God's job when it seems like what God promised is not happening as quickly as we would like. Whether it be Abraham having Ishmael or God's people desiring a king, we often get less than God's best when we refuse to rest in the preparation steps and his promises.

Our rebellious members often jump and twitch towards things that are good instead of things we know are God. The truth of the matter is that divine intervention is out of our control. We must trust the plans, preparations, and even the tightly bound positions that God places us in, knowing that if we can submit wholeheartedly to the tightly bound position, at the right time, God will turn us loose into the season called promise. After all, why would he leave us bound if, in his nature, he is the resurrection and the life?

Have you been prepared? Have you submitted to the healing process of the aloes and myrrh? Have you placed yourself in the right position to be clothed with a fresh and new identity? Have you been bound in a God way, so as to ensure your resurrection season? If not, start today. Your healing is as close as it has ever been. Your fresh start is on the horizon. Your purpose is about to be revealed and then unveiled. Your burial is declaring that *this is your season*!

As the day closed on Joseph and Nicodemus, what was bad seemed to only get worse. Jesus's dead body was, to most eyes, prepared for burial. It was over. The logical next step was to place it behind a stone in a borrowed grave, and for the person known as Jesus to be remembered though never seen again. However, these two men, the borrowed grave, the large stone, and the many heavy hearts had no idea that heaven was gathering its resources for the greatest rescue and the most significant moment in Christianity (and human history). And for the one in the tomb, resurrection was on its way.

Chapter 10

Lessons from behind the Stone: The Place of Transition

Now in the place where He was crucified, there was a *garden,* and in the garden there was a *new tomb* in which no one had yet been laid. So *there* they laid Jesus, because of the Jews' Preparation Day, for the tomb was nearby.

(John 19:41-42)

Life is full of lessons. Learning cannot be boiled down to only our experiences from high school or college. We cannot boil down all our education to math and reading. Life is an educator of epic proportion. Our circumstance and tragedy teach us continually. There is no better teacher than life. It is a great teacher because it perpetually gives us homework in way of our experiences. Our experiences, good and bad, provide a buffet of knowledge, wisdom, and understanding. If we allow ourselves to learn from them, we will glean lessons necessary for success in the next season of our lives.

This simple thought of life and its lessons provides a secondary and deeper insight: Our trouble brings as much knowledge and understanding as our triumphs. The reason I can say this with full assurance is because trouble in the kingdom of God is one of his most valuable professors. God uses this professor in our lives to teach us the most invaluable lessons about who he is and how he works. In your life, I can almost guarantee that the greatest revelations you have received about God and his ways have come riding in on the winds of trouble and pain. When our focus is on God and our minds are set "on things above" (Colossians 3:2), even in the middle of what seem like the worst moments of our lives, we are afforded the great privilege of gaining insights about who God is, the immensity of his strength, and what he can do.

Rest Stops

It is a difficult truth, but we often do not glean insights from trouble in life until after we complete a season of pain and a journey of preparation. After learning this valuable lesson over the course of my young life, I have just begun to understand that this is why God gives us invaluable seasons of rest. In these seasons of rest, if we are attentive, we can learn much about ourselves. We can learn about who we are becoming and what we have gained along the way or released from within us that we did not even know existed. I can say that most of what I have gained in understanding and knowledge about myself, I have gained only by going through the things I have gone through and coming out the other side.

God reveals our places of rest in our destiny as times to evaluate what we have learned from where we have come, and how we must apply what we have learned to where we are going next. I call this place the *hub of transition.*

The psalmist David declared that God, our great shepherd leads us beside still waters (Psalm 23:2). These still waters offer more than refreshment from our journey; they offer reflection for our future. These still waters are stopping points. They are the hubs of transition.

It is at these waters that we are afforded a chance to evaluate ourselves without the filters of the opinions and flattery of others. From here we are launched into our destiny.

"... still waters offer more than refreshment from our journey; they offer reflection for our future."

Hubs Have Many Looks

This is where our journey, navigating transition, has left us. We have come to the hub. We have come to the place of rest and evaluation.

I must tell you, it is a still place—a quiet place, and a necessary place. This is the next stop for you in your journey of navigating through transition. There must be a hub, a stopping place, in which you learn and apply all the things the previous season and place of life have revealed to you.

For Jesus, this place was a borrowed tomb. A borrowed tomb placed strategically in a garden. No one knew that the finality of his burial process would also serve as the place of solitude through which Jesus would spring forth in resurrection power.

Sometimes our hubs can look like tombs. I find such irony in this, that God in his sovereignty would use a literal resting place (the tomb) to illustrate the idea of a spiritual resting place (the hub of transition). Our resting places are not always pretty places. The goal of God concerning transition and your hub has nothing to do with pretty, comfortable, or even logical. It has everything to do with *your rest* and *his purpose*. The key questions to ask when approaching your "hub" of transition must be, *Can I rest here?* and *Can I evaluate here?*

Where is your hub? Have you taken the time to recognize the hub of your own transition? Perhaps the reason you have not moved forward has little to do with being over the past or being prepared for the future, and more to do with not evaluating who you have become and what you have learned. God is asking you to inspect the season of yesterday and the preparation of today to ensure you are equipped and empowered for the new season of tomorrow. He does not want you to simply lie there. God wants you to learn there. God needs you to get in that tomb and lie behind the stone.

Roll That Stone

As the last piece of linen was bound around the body of Jesus, there was only one thing left to do . . . place his prepared body behind a stone, in a tomb. Burial had arrived. I cannot imagine Joseph and Nicodemus's thoughts and emotions as they watched the stone roll over the borrowed tomb's opening. They undoubtedly knew they had done their job and could go no further with the body.

The only thing that remained was a season of introspection from behind a rolled stone and a borrowed tomb. To any masses or bystanders gathered, I am sure this moment seemed hopeless for their beloved Jesus. The stone was doing more than finishing his process, it was isolating him from the world. Certainly they thought that they would never see him again.

Lessons from behind the Stone

This moment in John 19 could be one of sadness. We no longer see Jesus. However, when life teaches us lessons, and trouble and tragedy are God's professors, this stone and borrowed tomb were just about to start class. If you listen with spiritual ears, you will hear the stone and tomb talking. They are teaching us valuable lessons concerning our God, our transition, and our future. Their truth will set us free.

Lesson 1: Isolation Is Initiation

In the world we live in, isolation is not a positive experience. We live in a world of constant connectivity. We can see the world, reach our peers, and do our work from the convenience of our cell phones and laptops. However, when these things are removed we feel anxious, out of the mix, and disconnected. Any way you slice it, to be isolated never seems good. However, in the kingdom, isolation is a positive thing.

Isolation is often the place of initiation into your destiny. In our cluttered and chaotic world, God has to have a way to get you alone so he can continue connecting you with your purpose. God uses your isolation to move you forward into the very purpose he has called you to accomplish.

"Isolation is often the place of initiation into your destiny."

This is seen over and over in the Bible. In fact, nearly every great man or woman of God we read about and celebrate has gone through intense seasons of isolation before God launched him or her forward.

- Moses lived out in the desert before leading the children of Israel out of Egypt.
- Joseph was trapped in a pit, Potiphar's house, and spent years in prison before becoming the prince of Egypt.

- David was a shepherd boy dwelling in lonely fields before being anointed king.

- Jesus spent forty days in the wilderness before beginning his ministry.

These are just a few of the many examples of isolation found in Scripture. God will use isolation not to merely make us feel lonely, but to make us into who we need to be to fulfill our purpose.

The tomb behind the stone was more than a resting place for the body of Jesus; it was the launching place of Jesus's destiny. The same is true for you. You ought to rejoice over seasons of isolation as they are the launching pad into the next level of what God has for you.

Lesson 2: Burial Seasons and Transition Are Often the Longest Seasons of Our Lives

How long? This is a question that quite naturally arises as the stone was rolled over the opening of the borrowed tomb holding the body of Jesus. It is the first question we ask while in the middle of transition. How long do we have to be here? How long will this transition take? There is no definitive answer to that question, but the burial season of transition does provide some insights.

Throughout Scripture, we are given the literal and prophetic time frame for how long Jesus would remain behind the stone: three days. For three days, he would remain in isolation, behind a rock, away from people. For three days he would remain seemingly silent, irrelevant, and unheard from. Three days.

Of the three major events of Passion Week—Jesus's death, burial, and resurrection—the lengthiest in time was his burial. Christ's crucifixion took only hours to accomplish, his resurrection was instantaneous, but his burial took three days.

What is God trying to teach us? What is God communicating? Is it possible that God is saying that the seasons of transition can be the lengthiest seasons of our lives? This is not a crazy idea. I believe this is quite likely.

We can see this laid out and played out over and over again throughout Scripture. Here are just a few examples:

- Forty days *between* the completion of the ark and the subsiding of the waters
- Twenty-five years *between* the promise of a son to Abraham and the birth of the promised son, Isaac
- Thirteen years *between* Joseph's dream and the dreamer being made overseer to Pharaoh in Egypt
- Forty years *between* the children of Israel's escape from Egypt and their possession of the Promised Land
- Fifteen years *between* the anointing of the shepherd boy David until the reign of King David
- Forty-two generations *between* the promise of the Messiah and the birth of Jesus
- Thirty-three years *between* the birth of the Messiah and the finished work of Jesus on the cross

Do you see it? Over and over in Scripture, moments of promise are followed by lengthy seasons of process. No matter the length, these seasons are always perfectly and divinely timed. Whether forty years or three days, hold on, keep learning, keep evaluating, and be patient. Know the design of God concerning the process of your transition is without mistake or error.

Lesson 3: It Is All About You

To the one behind the stone, three days must have felt like forever, but to heaven, it was the exact amount of time needed to fulfill God's Word and release God's purpose. Whatever the time frame of the completion of your transition, please know that it was and is the perfect amount of time to develop not just a new you, but the next you.

The new and next you are discovered through the stress of transition. As time goes by, we undergo a makeover of sorts. From behind the stone, unbeknownst to us, we are undergoing a metamorphosis in our thinking and actions. We are learning to make different decisions and attack life's opportunities in fresh new ways.

From behind the stone we learn that this moment in our transition is all about us. We bypass the thoughts and opinions of others and have

God's complete attention. When we truly get this truth, we will find that transition is more than our initiation into destiny or our preparation for purpose. We will find that it is even more than an evaluation of life lessons learned. Only from behind the stone do we see that transition is a transport for our own personal transformation.

"The new and next you are discovered through the stress of transition."

If this is true (and it is), we cannot help but emerge from this season as different people, with a fresh perspective and a new assignment. This hollow, empty tomb that serves as the hub of transition is also the womb by which Christ makes all things new. Simply said, there is a makeover in the middle of your going under.

Lesson 4: It Is Not Just Keeping Me In; It Is Keeping Them Out

It is here in the middle of our class with Dr. Tomb and Dr. Stone that Dr. Stone steps up to speak to us. He wants us to know that he is doing more than keeping you in; he is keeping unnecessary outside influences out.

God is using the stone as a way to hit the mute button on all the external voices in your life. The stone is a silencing sound barrier for the voices of fear, doubt, and unbelief. Left unchecked, these voices and influences will talk you out of your final stop in the transition process.

I am not sure why this happens, but it does. People will come out of nowhere to "lovingly" talk you out of what God has brought you into. These voices of "reason" often come in the form of family and friends. They all want what is best, and most are insanely sincere. However, I want to take a second here to instruct you. If God has brought you into this season, you must let him roll the stone away. You must allow him to silence every other voice and influence so you hear only his wisdom and that of those with his words in their mouths.

In these final moments of transition, the only threats to your deliverance are your own impatience and outside voices and influences of the world. How incredible it is to think that God cares so deeply about us that he takes this drastic and dramatic measure to ensure our success.

The stone is a final true barrier between your past and your future. It is a locked door to the former you and the former things. When God opens it up again, you will not be subject to fall to the same vocabulary and thoughts that had you and your mind bound. You will be an unstoppable person with an unstoppable purpose, backed by an unstoppable God.

Lesson 5: God Used It to Plant Me

The final lesson could be the most powerful. It does not come from our previous teachers. It comes out of a small detail in our passage of scripture in John 19. The disciple pens a key detail in John 19:41, stating that in the place where Jesus was crucified there was a *garden*. Yes, a garden.

How magnificent that in the middle of a garden with other buried seeds, God would bury his only begotten Son. The fact that this tomb was in a garden confirms that Jesus was not just a son . . . he was a seed! He was the seed of Abraham. Jesus taught this truth about himself when he said, "unless a grain of wheat *falls into the ground and dies, it remains alone;* but if it dies, it produces much grain" (John 12:24).

If Jesus is our example, then God is teaching us that at our hub of transition he has done more than bury us, he has planted us. Our planting is a twofold prophecy. On one level it lets us know *we will produce*, but on a second level it assures us we will also be *more mature* people, able to take on the next season with certainty.

This tomb is doing more than incubating you. It is germinating you. When you come out of this transition, you will be more than ready for your purpose. You will be mature enough to handle it.

You Are Almost There

As you read this, I truly hope you are finding a new hope. A hope that is persuading you that God is far from finished with you. Rest assured, from behind the stone you are gaining strength, refreshing your spirit, and finding restoration for your soul. Whether you are transitioning a ministry, a relationship, or a career, this imparted hope is a true and significant sign that your dream is still intact and God is in control.

Take a moment and evaluate yourself. What lessons have you learned about yourself? What have you gained in your transition? What are you becoming? Whatever it is, make no doubt about it, it has made you better and more complete for your purpose

You are almost there. Your transition is almost complete. So what now? There is one last step: Deliverance. Deliverance almost always comes on the heels of transition. It is the way out, not just out for a while, but for good; not out on the same level, but out in a new dimension. This is destiny step—a moment of purpose.

Turn the page now. The final chapter could help you experience your finest moment.

Chapter 11

Transitioned to Transition: The Next Transition

You made it! *After this?* Check. Transported? Check. Prepared? Check. Transformed? Check. You have not only been through the burial process, you have been through the burial season. There is only one thing left to finish your transition: You must be delivered.

I know that in some evangelical and charismatic circles, the word "deliverance" raises some serious questions. People immediately think of demonic activity, exorcism, spiritual warfare, demonic strongholds, and images of people being set free from spirits representing all types of awful behavior and substances. However, deliverance is most simply defined as, [1]"to be rescued or set free" (*Merriam-Webster* online). What a startling revelation. Deliverance has little to do with evil and much to do with good. Its definition implies a coming out, of sorts. It speaks of an exit or escape from imprisonment or a negative environment.

This is all your transition is missing: The moment when the divine hand of God rescues you and sets you free to enter the next season of life. The very thought of a life full of movement and purpose ought to drive your expectation and thankfulness toward God. God is about to do more than get you out; he is about to *let you out!*

However, this is not all God is going to do. Like a game show host to a contestant in the final moments of the show, God says, "But wait, there is more." God has more on his mind than just getting you out. The truth is, God will not bring you out and keep you out just to leave you wandering aimlessly in your newfound freedom and newfound self.

Walk, Do Not Wander

Nothing is more detrimental to mission and purpose than wandering. God does not deliver his people to leave them in the middle of nowhere, wandering, and wondering what is next. God will bring us out with the intention and agenda of moving us into the next step, place, and part of the journey: our purpose. He is intentional in making sure that once we are fully prepared and out of our last season that we move quickly to take the next step toward our destination.

What is God bringing you into? Do you know? Has it become clear yet? I assure you that all of the people, places, and impartations in your life to this point were more than preparation; they provide clues to the place you are heading next.

Do you remember the old children's show, *Blues Clues*? Even if you do not, I promise you, it is so important to assess your clues. Though each individual clue may mean something unique in and of itself, together they can all be perfectly woven together to work for your ultimate good.

Putting the pieces together will come naturally to a person with vision and a dream. However, at the end of the day, whether through prayer, the Bible, or even people, you must never forget the prophetic promises that God has spoken over your life. For all the things you have endured or gone through, it is crucial to hold on to each life-giving scripture the destiny filled Word of God has given you concerning your future. It is the nature of these prophetic promises to become the boundary within which you perfectly place all the pieces of your current transition, to bring out the complete picture of your new season. I will provide a biblical example of this.

A Quick Example

Outside of our passage, nothing could illustrate deliverance as the final part of transition better than the biblical story of Moses and the exodus of the children of Israel from Egypt.

Incubated and entombed in Egypt by God, the children of Israel grew despite their affliction and enslavement by Pharaoh. At the perfect time, God chose a deliverer and moment of deliverance. The goal was simple but twofold for the children of Israel. First, their leader and deliverer

(Moses) was to lead them out of Egypt. Second, they were to be led into the land of promise.

The best part of the story is simple: God was faithful to his promise and his word for the children of Israel. He promised deliverance for them, so they were delivered. Out of that promise, God perfectly and powerfully brought Moses out of his own transition and into his purpose as deliverer (a book in itself), and ushered the children of Israel out of the bondage of Egypt. As always, the deliverance was beautiful and divinely orchestrated. They were free, but not free to roam and do their own thing. A new master had enslaved them. They were bound, not by the Egyptians, but by the tenacious love of God. They were now prisoners of a destiny, a purpose, and a new land.

God is radically committed to you in the same exact way. He has freed you, not to wander aimlessly through life, but to bind you eternally to his perfect and eternal plan and will for your life. Until we get to our faraway home, our promised land (heaven), we will be led transition to transition so we can be moved from glory to glory (2 Corinthians 3:18). In the tomb of transition God is not making you a part of the plan, he is making the plan a part of you.

Timing Is Everything, and Timing Is His Thing

As we whittle away at the final moments of transition in our passage, we have seemingly stumbled into a new and powerful revelation. Unbeknownst to us, the body which had been moved, prepared, and sealed tight had been in the borrowed tomb for some time. Three full days passed and yet there was no real movement from heaven.

To be made whole, prepared, and ready, and yet hear or see no movement from God can be the most annoying part of transition. This is the point when most of us panic (which is understandable). You will be tempted to give up on what God said, and desert God's promise and plan if you lack faith and trust in his perfect timing.

The book of Ecclesiastes never instructs us to understand God's timing, but it emphatically tells us to understand that *there is a time for everything*! The last battle you will face in transition is the battle of understanding that true deliverance is not up to you. Deliverance is a part of God's perfect timing for delivering a God-sized purpose larger and higher than your own intellect and thoughts concerning your deliverance. When this revelation prevails, even in the darkest of tombs or bleakest of times, the peace that surpasses all understanding and time will ultimately take over, rendering you completely content in the current position and place God has you.

This may well be where you are right now. You have done everything right and nothing has happened. *Trust* God will do more than just sustain what he has started in your life; he will *finish* it.

When God Says Go

At this point in the process, if we did not know the end of the story, it would be fair to say it seemed as if God had given up. After all, Jesus did say, "My God, My God,, why have You forsaken me?" (Matthew 27:46).

Jesus had been dead for three days, and with every passing moment, fear, doubt, and unbelief filled the hearts of his disciples and enemies alike. It seemed all but over. However, to those with a spiritual ear and heavenly discernment, this story was far from over.

God was aligning the resources of heaven for the greatest transition of all time. With this transition of Jesus from the tomb, all of mankind would have an open door of deliverance and transition. All of heaven needed just one word from God . . . *Go!*

God's "Go" is always a response to our "Gone." Our obedience moves God to say, "Go." Over and over in Scripture the faith of people triggered a response from God. This last part of your move does not require *your move*, it requires *God's move*. Knowing this will steady you in the final anxious moments of your transition.

"God's 'Go' is always a response to our 'Gone.'"

This Is It

This part of the biblical narrative really needs no introduction. It has been the primary Easter sermon for hundreds of years. It has been portrayed in song, play, and drama in church services worldwide. This moment carries as much weight as our beginning point, *after this*. The moment to which I am alluding is none other than the resurrection of Jesus. Just recounting it from Scripture is awe-inspiring. Just think, within moments, what looked hopeless, over, finished, and done, became a moment of hope, redemption, peace, and so much more.

Before we see a rock rolled away, I want to recount what I see as the final moments of Jesus in the tomb. It is still dark. It is quiet in the garden. Jesus's body is still bound in the linens Joseph and Nicodemus fashioned. However, in the heavens above, God the Father (who had seemingly turned his back on Jesus), was actually at work on behalf of his only begotten Son.

In my own thoughts, I see God readying the cherub with detailed instructions for how and when to roll away the stone guarding the body of Jesus. I hear his voice letting the cherub know exactly what to say to Mary when she showed up there on resurrection day morning.

As heaven prepared for complete victory, I can see God looking for one final person. He was not searching for any angelic being, he was looking into his triune self. This conversation is with the Holy Spirit. Within this conversation were God's detailed plans which required the Holy Spirit to invade a dark and desperate tomb.

In this sovereign plan, the Holy Spirit would not just sit down beside Jesus, unwrap his burial clothes, and wake him up. In this holy plan, the Spirit of God himself would reside in the lifeless body of Jesus and raise it back to life. What a powerful concept—the Spirit would shift positions! No longer would he simply visit or rest upon those he encountered; he would live within them, empowering them to fulfill their purpose with divine *dunamis* (dynamite) power! This is our promise. This is our hope.

It Happened . . . Just Like That

I am not going to lie. This part is my favorite. For all the theory previously mentioned, the biblical reality resolves it all. In short: It happened . . . just like that. Early on that resurrection morning, the "Go" of God rolled the stone away (Luke 24:2), the Spirit of God was released into a borrowed tomb, the earth shook, and out came Jesus, resurrected and *alive!*

However, this was not the same Jesus. This Jesus had been changed. He had been glorified. This "new" and resurrected Jesus not only came out of his burial, he came out without limitation.

Later in Scripture (John 20-21) we see our risen Savior walking through walls, vanishing into thin air at a table after a journey on the Emmaus road (Luke 24:13-35), and ultimately ascended on a cloud on the Mount of Olives (Acts 1:9). No matter how you see it or read it, on the heels of his burial, Jesus the man was changed and transformed. He would never be the same.

The Same Spirit

I have saved the best news for last. I hope you are seated. The Bible is clear: The *same* Spirit who raised Jesus from the dead is *alive in you!*

> But if the Spirit of Him who raised Jesus from the dead dwells in you, He who raised Christ from the dead will also give life to your mortal bodies through His Spirit who dwells in you.
>
> (Romans 8:11)

Do you feel the weight and power of this verse of Scripture? What a revelation. Our postburial resurrection is not due to the work of a spirit similar to the Spirit who raised Jesus from the dead. The Bible tells us that the very same Spirit who raised Jesus from the dead has raised us to new life.

"On the other side of your burial season, your transitional moment is a glorious resurrection initiated by God through his Holy Spirit."

With this truth we are able to understand one final truth. If it was the same Spirit, then we will encounter the same life-changing, transformative results. On the other side of your burial season, your transitional moment is a glorious resurrection initiated by God through his Holy Spirit. This resurrection will destroy yesterday's limits and decimate former pains. We may wear the scars, but we will be liberated from the agony and pain. All that will remain is a testimony of God's faithfulness and a new, limitless life that will beg and plead with you to move forward and higher. You will be able to do more, and